Mommy Knows Worst

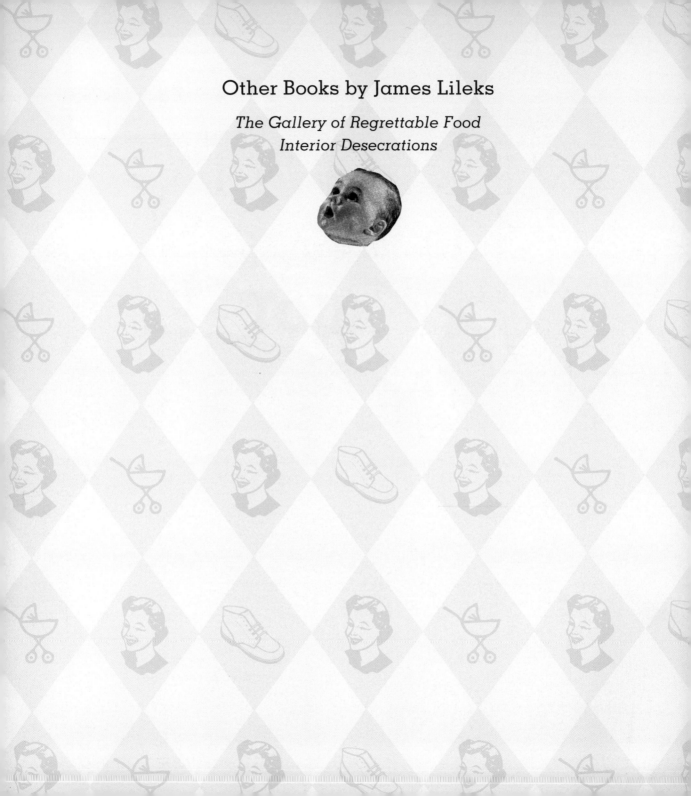

Other Books by James Lileks

The Gallery of Regrettable Food
Interior Desecrations

James Lileks

Mommy Knows

Worst

Highlights from the Golden Age of Bad Parenting Advice

THREE RIVERS PRESS · NEW YORK

Copyright © 2005 by James Lileks

All rights reserved.
Published in the United States by Three Rivers Press, an imprint of the Crown Publishing Group,
a division of Random House, Inc., New York.
www.crownpublishing.com

Three Rivers Press and the Tugboat design are registered trademarks of Random House, Inc.

Library of Congress Cataloging-in-Publication Data is available upon request.

ISBN-13: 978-1-4000-8228-5
ISBN-10: 1-4000-8228-5

Printed in the United States of America

Design by Kay Schuckhart / Blond on Pond

10 9 8 7 6 5 4 3 2

First Edition

ACCIDENTS... today are far more serious than usual because they interfere with winning the war—either directly (as in the case of the factory worker above) or indirectly (as in the case of the child, right, who, burning himself with matches, requires scarce medical care and may cause absenteeism of a war-working parent). Pg. 10

This book is dedicated to all those parents who figured things out for themselves and did a fine job, experts be damned.

And to all the kids who grew up hearing "Don't play with matches, dear. Hitler *loves* it when you burn yourself."

Most of all, it's dedicated to my daughter, without whom life would be dull and empty. Granted, I'd still have the wicked sports car I sold to buy the dull, safe SUV, but in the end, I'll take the kid.

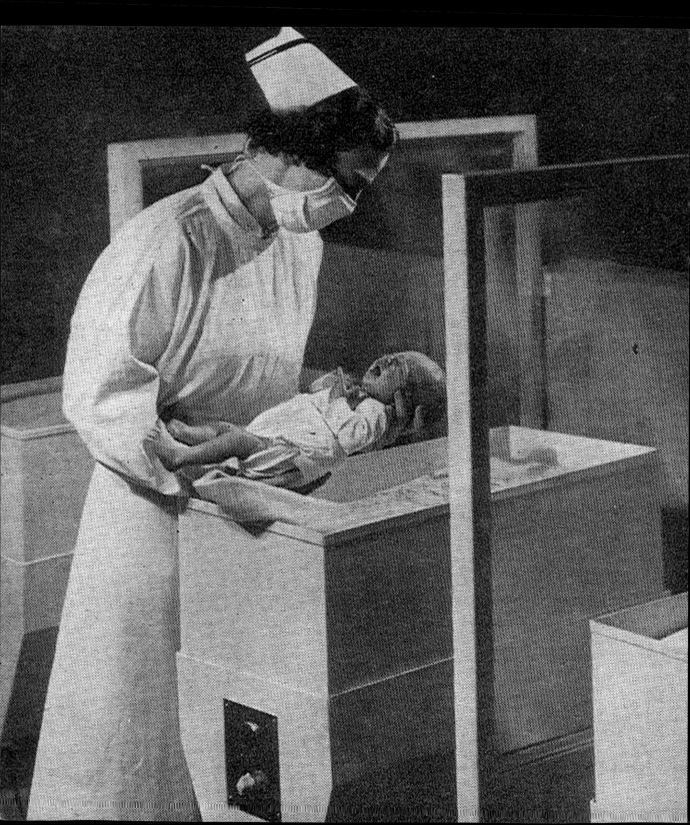

Contents

Introduction

This book is so unfair.

Really. Oh, some of the old advice seems odd — don't pick up the baby, feed them only bicarbonate of curd, swaddle them in asbestos during July, that sort of thing. But for the most part they got it right. How couldn't they? It's not as if having a child was an innovation peculiar to the 20th century. They had millennia of data on the matter, and there was a basic set of ideas that kept the human race multiplying at a reasonable rate. But when they were wrong, they were brilliantly wrong. Incandescently wrong. By the time the popular press and the government pamphlets got up to speed, most of the work consisted of undoing pseudoscience and superstitions: Why Your Baby Cannot Catch Rickets from Hearing a Crow in October, and that sort of thing. But they had their own blind spots, as every era does. As you'll see.

They also had their own limitations, which make them ripe fodder for smug moderns. Laugh if you will at the instructions for giving birth in the kitchen — and we hope you do; that's the point of this cruel endeavor — but some folk actually did have to give birth in the kitchen. No doubt modern hospitals will seem amusing and horrifying in three hundred years, after people are used to babies removed from the womb by teleporters while Mom has her nails done. No doubt our current manias and phobias will seem amusing someday, should history recall that America fell to the armies of China because they grew up hardened by pesticides while we poisoned our children with organic food. We'll see.

Until then, enjoy these glimpses of the olden days, when most of Mom's time was spent boiling bottles, dads were curious grumpy stubbled things that appeared in the house for no discernible reason, car seats resembled launching pads, and the children were spanked with hairbrushes for the sin of Constipation.

Let's begin.

The Good Old Days

Do Not Kiss Me

. . . or I will strangle you with my giant monkey-feet! Land's sakes, the kid could pick locks with those things. In any case, the heartwarming bib is a warning to people who have staggered from their deathbed to bestow one more sloppy, germy buss on the baby's mouth, unaware that sick people can transmit disease. Still, you suspect that other bibs in the series include "Do Not Make Prolonged Eye Contact" and "Do Not Pat Me After Meals, Let Me Accumulate Pent-Up Gas Until My Belch Knocks Crows off the Branches and My Farts Are Felt by Ships at Sea," and other children-should-be-born-but-not-otherwise-encouraged messages.

THE HOSPITAL IS A VERY GOOD PLACE TO HAVE A BABY

Just so you know. In case you had any doubts. It beats the kitchen, no? Because if you're going to have the baby in the kitchen you have to keep it clean, and that means keeping the chickens out. To say nothing of the goats or the hired man. No, wait until you feel a series of sharp pains in your baby-swell'd area, then walk calmly to the hospital. (Do not forget your head, as this woman appears to have done.) The hospital is a very good place to have a baby, because they have everything handy for emergencies, like fresh leeches and on-call phrenologists who can feel the bumps in your baby's skull and tell whether he suffers from moronism, Culler's syndrome, congenital bolshevism, or any other diseases that would fill you with shame.

And properly so.

THE HOSPITAL IS A VERY GOOD PLACE TO HAVE A BABY

A hospital is a good place in which to have a baby, because the hospital has everything handy with which to meet any emergency that may arise. Furthermore, the rest obtained following childbirth will help the mother to regain her health and strength more quickly.

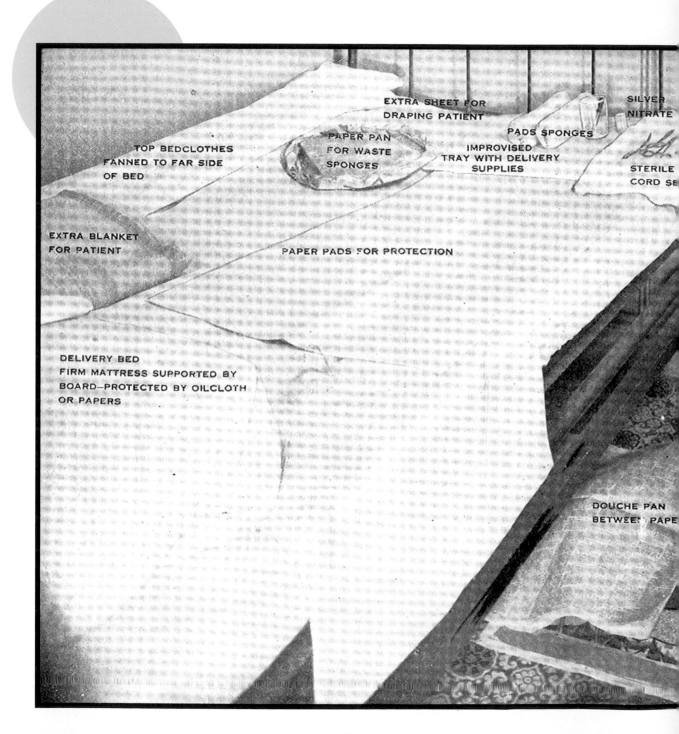

TOP BEDCLOTHES
FANNED TO FAR SIDE
OF BED

EXTRA SHEET FOR
DRAPING PATIENT

PAPER PAN
FOR WASTE
SPONGES

PADS SPONGES

SILVER
NITRATE

IMPROVISED
TRAY WITH DELIVERY
SUPPLIES

STERILE
CORD SE

EXTRA BLANKET
FOR PATIENT

PAPER PADS FOR PROTECTION

DELIVERY BED
FIRM MATTRESS SUPPORTED BY
BOARD—PROTECTED BY OILCLOTH
OR PAPERS

DOUCHE PAN
BETWEE PAPE

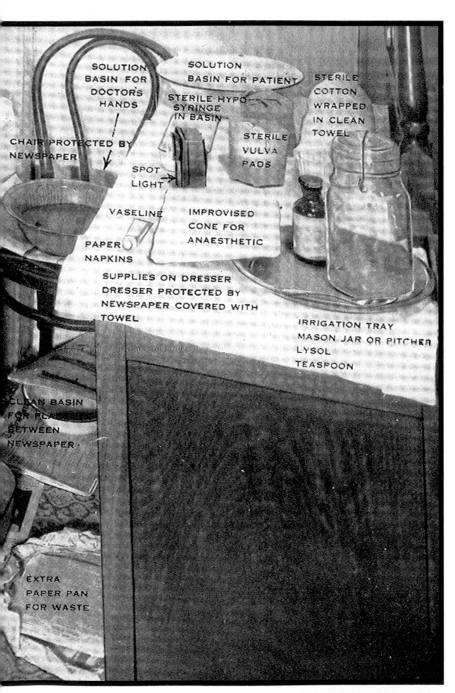

SOLUTION BASIN FOR DOCTOR'S HANDS

SOLUTION BASIN FOR PATIENT

STERILE HYPO SYRINGE IN BASIN

STERILE COTTON WRAPPED IN CLEAN TOWEL

CHAIR PROTECTED BY NEWSPAPER

STERILE VULVA PADS

SPOT LIGHT

VASELINE

IMPROVISED CONE FOR ANAESTHETIC

PAPER NAPKINS

SUPPLIES ON DRESSER
DRESSER PROTECTED BY NEWSPAPER COVERED WITH TOWEL

IRRIGATION TRAY
MASON JAR OR PITCHER
LYSOL
TEASPOON

CLEAN BASIN FOR FLAG BETWEEN NEWSPAPER

EXTRA PAPER PAN FOR WASTE

If you don't want to give birth in a hospital, there's always this: the home delivery room. Either that, or it's Jack the Ripper's dream house. The primary modern innovation seems to be the liberal use of newspapers. Let's examine the individual items.

Because when you want something to hold a half-dozen heavy sopping sponges, you naturally think of the editorial page with crimped edges.

"Chair protected by newspaper." What the chair is being protected from is not quite clear, and since the chair already looks like it spent a tour of duty as a prop in Lion Tamer's School, inordinate protection would seem superfluous.

"Clean basin for placenta between newspaper." So you don't have to look at it. This paper appears to have German warships, but you are free to select the martial implements of any aggressor nation. It's just a placenta.

> SUPPLIES ON DRESSER
> DRESSER PROTECTED BY
> NEWSPAPER COVERED WITH
> TOWEL

Fear not — the dresser dresser may look naked to the world, clad only in a towel, but beneath that nappy cotton exterior lies modern, wax-coated, oil-soaked, steel-bonded NEWSPAPER.

> EXTRA
> PAPER PAN
> FOR WASTE

This is here just so the doctor can shout, "Where the hell am I supposed to stand, exactly? What is the matter with you people? Who's delivering this baby, me or Hearst?"

Then again, perhaps the bedroom isn't right for you either. In that case . . .

KITCHEN
SINK

LIQUID
SOAP

HAND SCRUB

NURSE'S BAG
ON NEWSPAPER

CORNUCOPIA

PAPER
NAPKINS

HOT
BOILED
WATER
WITH
LADLE
↓

COOLED
BOILED
WATER
COVERED
↓

FOR CARE OF BABY
FOLDED BLANKET OR PILLOW
PROTECTED BY NEWSPAPER
COVERED WITH DIAPER
AND PINNED

CARE
FOR
BABY
NEAR
OPEN
HEATED
OVEN

RECTAL THERMOM-
ETER AND SCALES
ON PAPER NAPKIN

OIL SET IN
BASIN OF
WARM WATE

EMERGENCY

18

SET TUB OPEN
FOR WASTE SOLUTION

BABY
LOTHES
BLANKET
ARM BY
R BOTTLE

BABY'S TOILET
PER PAN   TRA
R WASTE

If you prefer, you can squeeze out the kid in the kitchen. Saves time, if you're one of those frugal farm folk who use the placenta as a soup base. First, pile the furniture in the corner, making it impossible for a doctor to get in. Then start foldin' papers, Ma! Let's examine the details:

At this point, you are free to suspect that the author was also the mind behind "Newspapers: the Key to Digestion" and "The Broadsheet Cure for Onanism" and other newspaper-related cure-alls.

Have you ever lain in bed with the kid a-crowning, hearing your husband bang around the kitchen shouting, "Goddammit, where's the cornucopia"? Then you understand why this book suggests you keep it out, in a handy place.

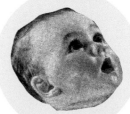

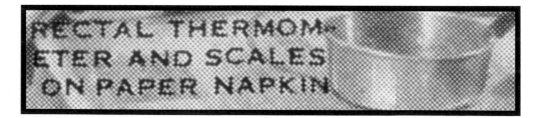

This is probably diner lingo for a very unpopular sandwich. *Two moons on a boat! Burn one with moo juice! Rectal Thermometer and Scales on a Paper Napkin!*

FOR CARE OF BABY
FOLDED BLANKET OR PILLOW
PROTECTED BY NEWSPAPER
COVERED WITH DIAPER

Again the mysterious faith in the protective power of newspapers! Against what? Was this the reason for the horrible death toll of World War I — French troops went over the top of the trenches, holding out copies of *Le Monde* in front of their torsos?

BABY'S
PAPER PAN
FOR WASTE

Bottom line: God forbid your due date falls during a slow news cycle. Best set aside a *Sunday Times*, just in case.

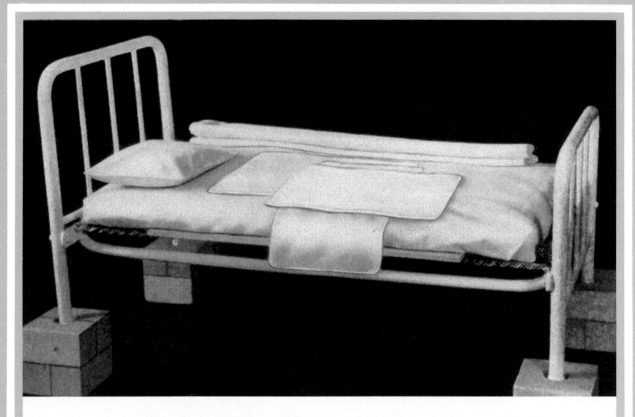

FIG. 62. Bed prepared for delivery in the home.

Nice image for the expectant mother to confront, eh? All that's missing are the handcuffs. I'm guessing the boxes around the legs are in case the water breaks. Really breaks. If you don't anchor the thing with lead weights, Mother just floats away.

> Mattress should be protected by a piece of rubber, waterproof paper, or just ordinary wrapping paper; it is then covered with a sheet drawn tightly and tucked in securely under mattress to avoid wrinkles. Bed pads are used for extra protection for the mother and the bed.

There would seem to be a great deal of difference between **rubber** and "**ordinary wrapping paper**," no? But at least the latter example lends a festive note to the proceedings. *She's crampin' up! Get out the Christmas paper! Don't bother with a bow!*

Apparently, giving birth without wrinkling the sheets was a great priority back then. *Lie still, dearie. Decent ladies leave nice smooth sheets. Creases are for harlots' beds.* One can understand why bed pads might be nice, since no one likes to bring new life into the world while laid out on a convict's cot, but "extra protection for the bed"? Did they expect the child to shoot out at Mach 3 and bend the railings?

BABY'S SLEEP

Ordinarily he should be taken up only to be fed, bathed, or changed.

Many people seem to think that a baby is a toy provided for the amusement of relatives and friends, and do not scruple to interfere with his very important business of growing up whenever they want to entertain or be entertained. In other words, it is considered perfectly proper to take him from his crib at any time when he is not sleeping for the purpose of exhibiting him, kissing, cuddling and bouncing him about.

This practice is a very pernicious one. The mother, perhaps, cannot be denied altogether the privilege of exhibiting her child to admiring friends, or of taking him up in order that she may lavish upon him her own caresses; but such disturbances should be reduced to a minimum, for they are very trying to the child's nerves and may even cause direct injury to his delicate little organs.

Still another harmful result may be to start the child in life with an exaggerated idea of his own importance. If his own common sense does not correct this error later on, it is not too much to say that it may land him eventually in an insane asylum, for the "exalted ego" is the most common delusion of the insane, and frequently has its origin in the first few years of the demented one's life. The Japanese are exceptionally free from this delusion. This is due to the fact that they do not pamper their infants. The early years are the most impressionable, and only too often infants are led astray with wrong impressions.

We cannot emphasize this enough: Leave the child alone. Is it crying? No. Is it soaking wet, or are its buttocks caked with its own abominable filfth? No. Leave it be. If you pick the child up and kiss it, there are two possible outcomes:

1. Internal organ damage caused by rough gusty "Bronx cheers" on the belly: spleen ruptures from a "harmless" game of gitchee-gitchee-goo.
2. Insanity, commitment, and the necessity of the parents staying indoors with the shades drawn for the rest of their lives, out of a decent sense of shame.

When in doubt, remember: *Nothing shreds a child's nerves like mother's disturbing caresses.*

Health & Hygiene

Tuesday Is Diaper Boiling Day!

CHICAGO'S HEALTH

The Diapers Should Be Boiled

Soiled diapers should be kept in a covered pail until washed. The diapers and other soiled clothing should always be washed, boiled and finally thoroughly rinsed.

The soiled wet diaper may have a strong smell of ammonia and may irritate or burn the baby's skin. Occasionally this may be due to sickness or wrong feeding, but most commonly it is caused by germs growing in the diapers and clothing as a result of wrong methods of washing.

If the baby's buttocks are sore, boric acid powder may be sprinkled on the boiled wet diapers before hanging them up to dry. If the buttocks stay sore, it is best to see the doctor.

Bed linens should be boiled. The rubber sheeting should be washed daily and aired. The mattress should be taken outdoors and aired and left in the sun every day for several hours, if possible.

The crib is kept clean by washing it thoroughly once a week.

167

As this illustration demonstrates, you should fill a small trough with boiling water and spend a miserable July afternoon moving the horrid sodden mass around, keeping one hand free to bat away the blueflies, until the diapers have dissolved completely. Then weave new ones. If the baby's buttocks become sore from insufficiently clean diapers, boil the baby in a solution of boric acid. The bed linens should also be boiled on the hour, and in between boiling sessions, take care to boil the mattress, drag it outside, and let it air. In the winter, you will have to break it into pieces with a sledgehammer if it freezes, but you can sew it together with string (boil for two hours ahead of time) and restuff it with handfuls of your own hair, which you have been pulling out by the handful lately. Because you don't know how much more of this you can take. Tomorrow: disassembling the crib and boiling the slats. Wednesday: boiling the dog. Thursday: boiling the pots you use to boil things. Friday: impregnation.

LIFE SUCKS

CARE OF THE BABY'S MOUTH; THUMB SUCKING

Most doctors now prefer that the healthy baby's mouth should be let alone till the teeth come, as harm is often done to the delicate membranes by trying to wash the mouth every day. When teeth appear they should be cleansed every day with boiled white rags or absorbent cotton. Two-year-old tots may be taught to use a soft, small brush.

The young baby's mouth stands a poor chance of keeping healthy unless *everything that goes into it* is clean. The nursing mother should cleanse her nipples before and after each feeding with boric acid solution. Pacifiers are injurious and often dirty, and their use should never be begun. The habit of thumb sucking often persists till the mouth is deformed. Break the habit up, no matter what effort it costs you. With young infants, try putting a mitten on the hand, or wrapping the favorite finger with adhesive plaster. Rubbing the finger of an older child with garlic or liquid bitter aloes is harmless, and often breaks up thumb sucking.

There's nothing wrong with boric acid, except for the acid part; no matter how mild the stuff may be, this passage still seems to suggest that nursing mothers should plunge their teats into something one associates with the innards of automotive batteries.

The injunction against pacifiers is wise. The authors of this tract would be horrified to see the array of plugs sold for the Gerber Hole in the 21st century — why, with their gay colors and better-than-nature nipples (It's not like Mom's was an inch long and formfitting to the roof of the mouth.

Well, not at first, anyway.), it would be odd for a child not to want a pacifier, and cruel for a parent to withhold one. Personally, I can't stand the things. They send the wrong message: Life Sucks. They drop on the floor, and you feel compelled to boil them in — well, boric acid. When lost, it is a matter of national calamity, and the child is bereft until replugged; parents will do anything to halt the wails, even if it means retracing your steps for the last 48 hours and putting on a wet suit to plumb the depths of a McDonald's Dumpster. Look carefully at the film of refugees streaming from Paris on the eve of the German invasion; you will see a few families stumbling back toward the city. They are going back for the nuk.

It's easier to break your kids of the habit of smoking. In fact, if you are going to get your child a pacifier, get one that dispenses small amounts of nicotine; later you can put them on the patch. So imagine my delight when Child did not want the nuk. Showed no interest. Spat it out as the palliative it truly is. Didn't even suck her thumb. No, she was content to gnaw on the dog's tail when she wanted some oral satisfaction. But what if she had demanded the pacifier? What if she had become a thumbsucker? At some point you have to break the habit, lest it change the baby's very nature:

The period of teething used to be particularly dreadful. Long before teeth were expected, fond mothers, believing that early teething was a mark of superior intelligence, rubbed the babies' gums with silver thimbles. But even bachelor uncles knew that any child, while teething, was liable to be sick with a fever, a "teething rash," an intestinal upset, and often a convulsion. No doctor was needed to make a diagnosis because anyone could look in a baby's mouth and even though no offending teeth could be seen, the child was teething nevertheless and was given a teething ring to help assuage the pain. The final proof came when the gums were lanced, for cures followed lancing as the night the day. It is very surprising indeed that science has been able to overcome this belief in so short a time. Today we have gone to the opposite extreme and every medical student is taught that attributing diseases to the teeth is about the most dangerous habit in the whole field of medicine on the ground that one is liable to overlook and neglect the real cause of the complaint. Lancing the gums in order to cure diseases has gone with the bustle.

This self-congratulatory entry hails from 1943, when most people had come to accept — however grudgingly — that "purple fever" could not be cured by smearing the baby with cigar ash and cat saliva. It's a nice window into the era of medicine when both doctors and bait salesmen came to your door with a pail of leeches. The article also debunks the "Second Summer," a period when children regularly got the heaves or blurts or some interminable combination of both. Never wean a child during Second Summer! Why? Silly woman — the sun affects the magnetic properties of your breasts; every grandmother knows that. As it turns out, the "Second Summer" ailments were usually due to bad food. Once the kid was off the spout, he was drinking milk from foamy-mouthed cows and eating pieces of meat that had so many germs you'd actually get mail addressed to E. Coli, Esq. If you think we're exaggerating, well, the following pages feature are some prime remedies from the good ol' gum-lancing days.

Flaxseed Poultice

INTO a pint of boiling water stir flaxseed, also known as linseed, until it forms a paste just thick enough to flow from a spoon; add a tablespoonful of sweet-oil or glycerin; spread it one-half inch thick between two layers of cheese-cloth; apply where directed, and cover with a layer of cotton, warm flannel, or oiled silk. If the part to be poulticed is anointed with sweet-oil or vaseline before the poultice is applied, no blisters will be raised.

Mustard Poultice

To make a mustard poultice take three teaspoonfuls of mustard and six teaspoonfuls of wheat-flour, add two teaspoonfuls of sweet-oil or glycerin and enough warm water to make it into a thick paste. Spread between two layers of cheese-cloth, and apply to the part directed, after anointing the part with vaseline. This poultice can be left on only a few minutes and the skin should again be anointed with vaseline or dusted with cornstarch.

Mustard Foot-Bath

To give a mustard foot-bath, tie one tablespoonful of mustard into a cheese-cloth bag. Let this soak for a few minutes in a foot-tub containing two quarts of warm water, temperature 102° F. The feet should be immersed to above the ankles for about two minutes. On removing the feet, place them near a hot-water bottle or wrap them in a warmed towel.

Is this good? Or bad? Do you want the blisters perhaps to "draw out" the "blood vapors" or "liver wraiths," or do blisters interfere with the healing power of viscous flaxseed? It's hard to say, since this book gives no indication what the poultice is for. It's just one of those things you slap on the kid when they have a croupy spell, perhaps. But what if it doesn't work? Kick it up a notch:

Mustard has lost its reputation as the Great Healer; it's pretty much retired to a life as a condiment. But back then it was regarded as a medicine with such power that its healing properties could fight their way through cheese-cloth and a thick impasto of petroleum jelly. If you applied it directly, the child would probably spring up and start belting out light operetta tunes. But what if this didn't work?

At this point, the parent is tempted to take the next step and introduce relish and onions to the foot-bath, but only if the physician has directed you to do so. Or the grocery clerk. Nevertheless, not all infectious diseases of the lung respond to foot-baths, so you may need a turpentine stupe.

Frightened is the mother whose child falls ill without a can of paint thinner in the medicine cabinet.

Which brings us to perhaps the most inefficacious remedy encountered thus far.

Thus was pneumonia cured: by sewing. Your doctor would write out a prescription: six yards of cotton, two spools of thread, a bolt of cheesecloth. Repeat as necessary. Perhaps the prudent mother prepared a full set of sickness garments ahead of time — the pneumonia jacket, the diphtheria ascot, the influenza corset, and the constipation dickey.

Turpentine Stupe

A turpentine stupe is made by adding one-half teaspoonful of spirits of turpentine to one pint of boiling water and mixing thoroughly. Dip two thicknesses of flannel into this turpentine and water and wring out until it does not drip. Apply as directed and cover with a large piece of cotton or oiled silk.

Pneumonia Jacket

A pneumonia jacket should be shaped like baby's sleeveless shirt. A layer of cotton is placed between a layer of cheese-cloth and one of oiled silk. The edges are turned in and the three layers basted together. The shoulder seams or straps may be sewed together or tied with tapes. The front is closed by means of tapes sewed on either side. The jacket is worn with the layer of cheese-cloth next to the skin. If the skin is moist, alcohol sponging is necessary before a new jacket is applied. Two jackets should be made so as to have a change when one gets moist.

Protruding Ears

Some babies have prominent ears and this may be a source of annoyance to mothers. A band of porous cloth or net to prevent babies' ears from sticking out may be used. A pattern for such a band is shown below.

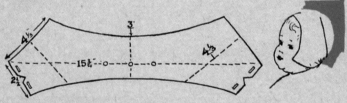

The ends are sewn together at the notched edges and tape is attached to the corners.

Net caps for holding the ears back can also be bought. They cover the whole head, are cool and comfortable.

Prominent ears, a source of annoyance. You can well understand why. You're having the ladies over for tea and whist. This is the first time Clara has joined the group, and her sister knows a fellow whose cousin is dating a Vanderbilt, and everyone is atwitter to hear all the details. She intimated that she might bring an item from the Vanderbilt house, if you can imagine such a thing. If it is a hatpin, the girls have all vowed to prick themselves with it. Why, it would almost make them honorary Vanderbilts, wouldn't it? In a way, it would.

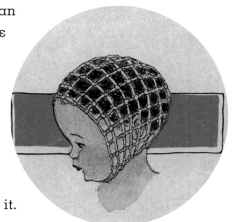

The afternoon is a smashing success. Anna — she's married to a simply beastly man, but he's one of the Kuppers, you know, the iron and smelt Kuppers of Birmingham. Anyway, she was describing a bonnet she wore to visit a friend in the hospital, poor thing, women troubles, and — "say, weren't you in the hospital?" she asked. And you went red. Yes, you admitted, you were. A spot of pregnancy, but it's run its course. And all the girls shrieked and clapped their hands and wanted to see the baby, now, this instant! What could you do? You rang the bell for the nursemaid, who got the baby from wherever she keeps her, and brought her in.

They fell silent when the baby was brought in, smiled politely, and insisted she was just lovely. *It's a he, you said, and I know what you're thinking. Those prominent ears do annoy me so.*

"Haven't you heard?" Clarice piped up. "They're doing wonderful things with Ear-Binding Head Nets these days; you really ought to try one."

You had the manservant pick one up, and the child seems to like it.

Well, if he's complained, the nursemaid hasn't said anything.

Diphtheria's Death Month
is November

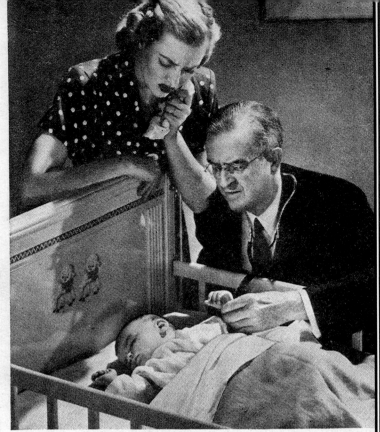

Among children under five, diphtheria's death rate is highest. If all little children were properly immunized, diphtheria would be wiped out entirely!

Deaths from diphtheria usually are 10% to 50% higher in November than in any other month, government records show.

And nearly two-thirds of those who will die from diphtheria this month will almost certainly be little children—under five!

These deaths will be *especially* tragic because they could have been *prevented*—by immunization. In New Haven, Conn., where almost every child has been immunized, diphtheria has been practically *eliminated*.

If *your* baby is six months of age or over—and has not been immunized against

---

This card tells you *when*

With this card, you know just when to take your child to the doctor for the immunizations—not only against diphtheria, but against *other* preventable diseases.

This card shows *what diseases* your child should be immunized against and at *what ages*.

No busy mother can *possibly* keep track of this herself. Immunizations against different diseases are given at different ages ... some diseases require repeated immunizations—and safety periods vary! It's like a Chinese puzzle!

So . . . phone ahead and make reservations?

My stars, what a day-brightener this must have been. You open the mag to look for Thanksgiving ideas, and you're hit with the **DEATH MONTH.** But it serves a purpose. It advises mothers to get a card — free! — that helps them keep track of crucial vaccinations. The doctor will help you, of course. Oh, if only it were as easy as a Persian riddle or a Bulgarian rebus, but no! It's as hard as a Chinese puzzle!

Sun & Air

Sun Good, Burn Bad

If there's one thing the old books agree upon, it's the importance of leaving young children to bake in the sun, preferably until they have attained the hue of a pot roast. It's the most striking example of how things have changed in recent years. If Coppertone today ran an ad with a brown little sprite getting her pants yanked off by a dog, they'd be visited by authorities from a variety of jurisdictions, but that ad summed up the prevailing attitudes: Sun Good, Burn Bad. Spray the tots with some goop and let 'em romp, and as long as the flesh didn't peel off in strips as wide as the daily paper, fine. Now, of course, parents regard the sun as the big giant flaming ball of death, and will not let children stand near the window unless they are covered in gunk whose SP rating is equivalent to roofing tar. Any parent at the pool who doesn't cover the child with a quart of cold, oily sunblock gets hard looks and tut-tuts from the other moms — why don't you just give her a CIGARETTE while you're at it, they might say. ("Because she didn't finish her grapes," you would sensibly reply.) There's also sunblock for the scalp, which seems eminently sensible — until you recall the notable lack of skull-burn you suffered as a carefree child. But who are you to argue; on it goes. Within a few years, we will be spraying sunblock into the children's mouths, lest some stray rays enter the oral cavity and bounce around in their head, spattering their lethal photons hither and yon.

36

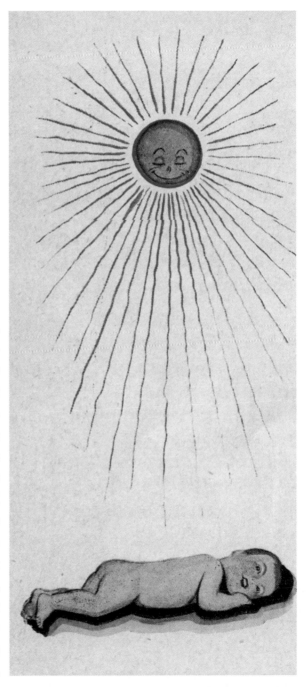

Back then, however, the sun was seen in a role that was almost downright helpful. And for good reason. It giveth unto thee the vitamin D, which was in short supply in the daily diet. Before gummi vitamins, before year-round orange juice, before bread fortified with so many minerals you could use a slice to find the magnetic pole, children suffered from diseases such as rickets. But since the body could turn sunshine into vitamin D, parents were encouraged to stick the kid in the sun every day.

The illustration here is typical, right down to the lines we all somehow know mean "sunlight." Inasmuch as they're dark, and visible.

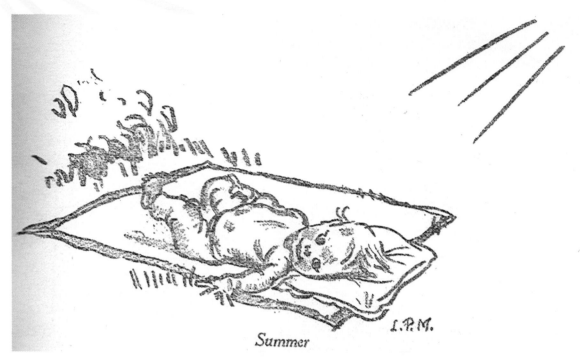

Summer

L.P.M.

L.P.M.

If you start in the spring, orient yourself properly. Look for a spot where the lines are falling from the sky, and hold the baby so it can catch the rays in its chubby little hands; this promotes dexterity. Rotate the baby to assure even basting; if the rays accumulate on the ground around you, use the thinner ones to floss between the toes.

Fall

By fall the child should answer to the name "Mahogany." Do not be alarmed if large, jagged pieces of skin detach when the breeze comes up and accumulate around the sandbox.

Winter

Wintertime is still sunbath time! Find the window through which the black lines bounce off and fall to the ground; save them for later, in case there is a depression and sunlight becomes so expensive only the rich can afford it. Roll the baby under the window and open it up. Winter air is healthful air, and this picture is an ideal prescription for infant health. Unless, of course, there was just an explosion at the knitting needle factory and those aren't sunbeams after all.

Ah, but sun is not enough. A child must also have air. Even in those rudimentary days, studies showed a direct correlation between total lack of air and infant mortality. It wasn't enough to supply air, however; it had to be good air. None of this breeze-in-the-tanning-factory stuff. Preferably, windows should be left open enough to admit air and discourage predators. But what if you lived in a tenement that had but one window per room and did not have cross-ventilation?

Trust science to have the answer.

BOGGINS' OPEN-AIR SLEEPING COMPARTMENT
View from the Street.

Sales dropped off after the Lindbergh kidnapping.

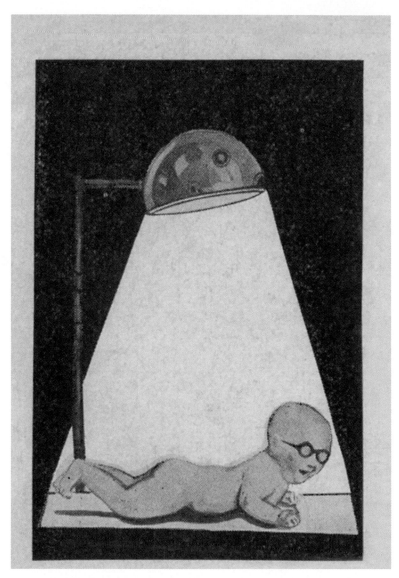

Warning! Use of indoor lights may turn child into an evil supergenius, as seen here. If the child develops the telltale symptoms of Evil Supergeniushood — the black-rimmed glasses, the cruel and mocking mouth — discontinue use of light *immediately*. Unless, of course, he comes up with a great plan for hijacking the German zeppelin fleet to strike terror among the capitals of the world; if his logistics are sound, go for it.

General Advice

THE CRIME OF SOOTHING SYRUPS

Of the pleasures that await a new mother, that first shot of booze may be numbered among the favorites. Ever since the little plastic wand said *plus*, she has gone without. No wine with a meal. No beer on a hot summer day. Don't even think of driving through the wine country, unless you keep a constant speed above 50 MPH; any slower and you can actually feel the baby shed brain cells.

It's a significant change from the golden age of oh-what-the-hell pregnancies of the '50s and '60s, where a mom could put back a Schlitz or three without worrying that Child Protective Services would charge her with Zygote Abuse. And it's a great distance from the early part of the 20th century, when the author of *How to Raise the Baby* dedicated the ominous-sounding CHAPTER X to an unusual topic: Don't use dope to shut up the little brat so you can go to the theater. In this excerpt, the author manages to express contempt for everyone — society, animal welfare do-gooders, careless fools with medical degrees, pinheaded ninny-moms, evil old dope-pushing crones — but she reserves her most potent ire for the dimwits who give their children laudanum, Chinese opium, and other "hell broths" the patent medicine industry cheerfully bottled for your stuporific enjoyment.

It's unfair sometimes to tut-tut at the past for not knowing what we know now, but this is different. How stupid were they? *This* stupid.

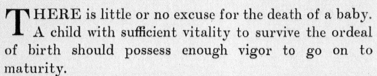

CHAPTER X

The Crime of Soothing Syrups

"And be these drugging fiends no more believed
That keep the word of promise to our ear,
And break it to our hope!"

THERE is little or no excuse for the death of a baby. A child with sufficient vitality to survive the ordeal of birth should possess enough vigor to go on to maturity.

Yet during the War it was estimated that the life of a soldier in the trenches was safer than that of a baby in its cradle. The little creatures fall victims by the thousands to the ignorance and sometimes the criminal neglect of mothers, the incompetence of physicians, and the general indifference and neglect of a social body which cares more, apparently, for safeguarding the health of baby pigs and cows than for the welfare of human infants.

Of all the crimes that are committed against baby-hood one of the most flagrant is the drugging of the little ones by means of the various hell-broths known as "teas," "soothing syrups" and the like.

The most charitable thing that can be said of a woman who will pour one of these decoctions down the throat of her helpless infant is that she is sinning through igno-rance. None the less is she committing a terrible crime, and none the less will Nature exact the penalty of her wrong-doing, possibly from herself, but certainly, alas! from her tiny victim.

[96]

THE CARELESS MOTHER

But not even the questionable excuse of ignorance can be pleaded in the case of thousands of women who disgrace the name of mother. These women, lacking the love, patience, and wisdom of the true parent, will "quiet" baby at any cost.

The peevishness of the child may be the outcome of uncomfortable clothing, improper food, underfeeding or overfeeding, want of exercise, need of fresh air and sunshine, or neglect in general. But to such conditions the mother of the type in question gives little or no thought.

Usually of the fairly well-educated middle class, she lives for the bargain counter, the matinee and the "movie" theatre. Her home is incidental to, rather than the pivotal point in, her life. And her shallowness and selfishness prompt her to dislike its duties and detest its encumbrances, including the "squalling brat."

So when the wail of the unhappy child annoys her, she does not seek to remove the cause of its unhappiness. Instead there is a visit to the cupboard, the production of a bottle, the prying open of a small, feverish mouth, and the baby sinks into an uneasy, drug-induced slumber. There are even mothers who do this with a clear consciousness of the fact that they are "doping" their children.

BECAUSE GRANDMOTHER USED TO DO IT

There is a third species of drug-administering mother who will reply to your remonstrances by asserting that "mother always used that 'tea' for her babies," or "grandmother raised all her children" on some other ungodly brew. In such instances you will invariably

[97]

find that the family so "raised" can, as the doctors say, demonstrate a variety of nervous diseases, chronic dyspepsia, crankiness and other tokens of unbalanced organisms.

All this is lost on the thoughtless mother, however, whose undeveloped brain only permits her to do that which her predecessors did. Which is also the way of sheep, you will remember. These drug-administering mothers are numbered by thousands.

Dr. Wilbur Hale, who for a long period was the head of one of London's famous hospitals for children, and who had an international reputation as an expert on infant maladies, was once asked to state the dominant impression that he had received from his years of practice. His reply was:

"The everlasting stupidity of the average mother."

This was a severe and perhaps too sweeping generalization, but it must be remembered that Dr. Hale was constantly in touch with the tiny victims of parental blunders or worse.

EITHER STUPID OR WICKED

Still, it goes without saying that the mother who will tamper with the exquisitely delicate and fragile machinery of her baby's system by clogging it with narcotic poisons of any kind is crassly stupid, if indeed she be not fiendishly wicked.

Every year millions of bottles of the stuff that is supposed to bring about "natural refreshing sleep" are sold, and thus the bodies and brains of more than a million of babies are irretrievably injured.

It is a deliberate lie to say that "natural, refreshing

[98]

sleep" can ever be brought about by a narcotic, for no drug ever did or ever can achieve this result.

The active element in most syrups is laudanum, a form of opium, the flavor being disguised by essences scarcely less harmful, and the whole "digested" in a heavy sugar solution. Pleasant stuff truly to put into a baby's stomach—an organ that is intended to receive, and adjusted to digest, but one thing—its mother's milk.

Some years ago, a wholesale and systematized series of child murders was unearthed in Paris. For a consideration of a few francs an unwelcome baby could be sent to a *maison des enfants* kept by a couple of old women. In due season the child would die. When the police raided the place, some cases of "soothing syrup" were among the things seized. One of the hags who confessed said that it was administered to the little victims because it was safe, sure, and could be bought anywhere!

Paregoric is another opium-laden drug that is very dangerous indeed. In this connection it is proper to call attention to the fact that many a woman who lifts up eyes and hands in righteous horror at tales of Chinese opium dens and their degraded inmates will, nevertheless, administer opium to her baby, for paregoric is opium. And there is ample medical testimony to prove that a large proportion of the "dope" fiends of our own race are what they are because of the love of the drug implanted in them in infancy by their mothers. Can anything be more terrible than this?

Well might some of our babies lisp, "From such mothers, good Lord, deliver us!"

THE CRIME OF SYRUPS —
REPEALED!

Yes, *it's Super Anahist*, the *delicious* expectorant, the precursor to the Nyquil Smoothie. Make it special, Moms: crushed orange-flavored baby aspirins serve as festive sprinkles.

WARNING: Side effects include irregular eyebrows, loss of canine teeth, pupils the size of pencil points, and a record with the juvenile hall when he starts breaking into drugstores and ice cream parlors.

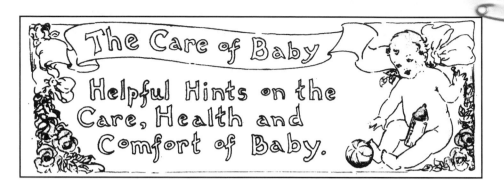

The Care of Baby

Helpful Hints on the Care, Health and Comfort of Baby.

Bowel Movement. See that the bowels move every day. Never let a day pass without a good movement.

Preferably something reminiscent of later Beethoven.

Air. Give the baby pure air day and night. Avoid dust, drafts, overheated rooms, crowds and unnecessary contact with colds and other germ diseases. The belief that children should have measles, whooping-cough, etc., "early, and get done with them" is wrong. The after-effects of these diseases often keep children weak for many years.

Doctors agree; air is good, no matter what time of the day, unless you want them to die "early, and get done with it."

Warmth. Keep the baby's hands and feet warm, and its bowels warmly protected with wool.

"Externally" will suffice.

As to Medicine. No mother would quiet her child with a blow on the head, nor should she stun her baby with the opium and morphine of soothing syrups. Many babies have been killed by medicine given to stop a fretful cry. Any medicine that promises to quiet a baby or put it to sleep should be shunned like poison.

Because it is, you know, POISON. To sum up what we've learned thus far: Give the baby air and don't stun it with opium. Let us continue:

> *Rest.* All young infants are extremely nervous, so avoid exciting them, playing with them, or handling them too much. Do not trot, shake or bounce the baby. Do not start the bad habit of walking the floor. Baby's bones are soft for a long time, and even holding the baby habitually may cause spinal curvature. A little handling and petting rests the baby, but most of the time young infants should lie quietly in bed till strong enough to sit alone and play.

Mom! This is the future! Hello! THEY DON'T KNOW WHAT THEY'RE TALKING ABOUT!

Does this even make sense to you? They have soft bones? Okay, try this: Bend one. Doesn't work, does it? They're not made of pipe cleaners. Trust me here: We've been holding our babies constantly for twenty years, and the streets are not choked with young adults bent over as though they bear a great invisible burden. TROT that baby! Dare we even suggest you PLAY with them. A happy, well-bonded baby will be more likely to grow up well-adjusted and con-nected, and less likely to regard the world with sullen suspicion and a gnawing need to satisfy needs never met in the crib —

On the other hand, your 1915 baby will be hitting adulthood in in the Great Depression, so maybe toughening it up from the git-go isn't such a bad idea. Okay, put him back in the cradle. Leave the room.

This is the future. Sorry we bothered you.

The BABY'S DAY
"Clock-Wise"

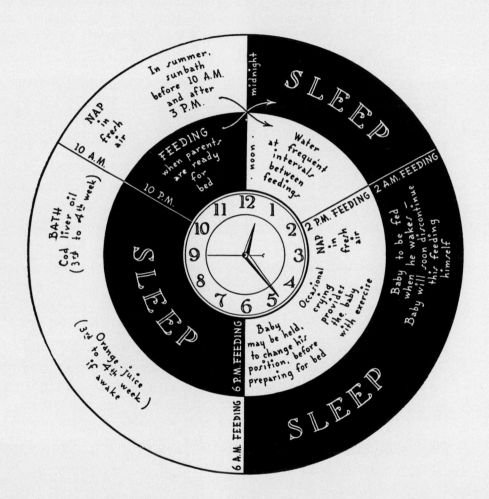

Behold: a simple device for sending postpartum depression women completely over the edge.

It seems to suggest that orange juice should be given from 6 A.M. to 10 A.M., so expectant parents should plant the grove now.

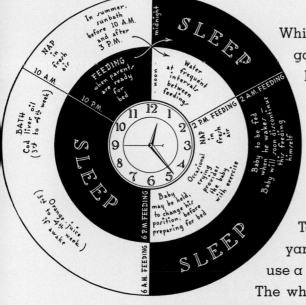

The wheel contains the following labels:

SLEEP

In summer, sunbath before 10 A.M. and after 3 P.M.

NAP in fresh air

10 A.M.

BATH Cod liver oil (3rd to 4½ week)

(3rd to 4th week if awake) Orange Juice

10 P.M.

FEEDING when parents are ready for bed

midnight

soon

Water at frequent intervals between feeding.

2 A.M. FEEDING

NAP in fresh air

2 P.M. FEEDING

Baby to be fed when he wakes; Baby will soon discontinue this feeding himself

Occasional crying provides the baby with exercise

Baby may be held, to change his position, before preparing for bed.

6 P.M. FEEDING

6 A.M. FEEDING

SLEEP

SLEEP

While the child attempts to metabolize the latest gallon of juice, give it a two-hour bath in cod liver oil. If you can pick the baby up without him squirting out of your hands like a bar of soap in the shower, he's not oiled up enough. After 10 A.M.? Consult the wheel: "In summer sunbath before 10 A.M." Which is why they put that helpful advice at 11 o'clock high. If you failed to heed the wheel today, no matter. Tomorrow you can take the child out in the yard, place him in a trough of cod liver oil, and use a funnel to administer the daily gallon of juice.

The wheel provides other nuggets of scientific wisdom: A "nap in fresh air" is good, and provides a welcome change from a nap in a room that has been sealed since Lincoln was shot. "Occasional crying provides the baby with exercise" comes at 4 P.M., which is just about when Mother has had enough and is eyeing the "nerve tonic" bottle with grim despair. Let him cry, Mother; it is nature's way of firming the lungs. Have some codeine. Finally, do not worry that you are spoiling the baby by touching it from time to time: "Baby may be held, to change his position, before preparing for bed." As for how long you may hold your baby before he becomes the sort of weak, needful, neurasthenic young man Teddy Roosevelt would hold in frank contempt, let your instincts be your guide.

Things Which Are Bad for the Baby

1. All kinds of candy, ice-cream, tea, coffee, and cakes.
2. A bottle nipple, a crust, or a bone tasted by someone else before giving it to the baby.
3. Using for the baby without washing, a spoon or glass, or cup, that someone else has used.
4. Sucking air from a partly-filled or an empty bottle.
5. Dirty playthings and toys.
6. Sneezing or coughing near the baby or letting a person with a cold come near the baby.

This selection of wise advice comes from an early-20th-century pamphlet handed out by the state of Pennsylvania. It's hard to argue with them. A baby should not be given coffee, or it will begin to request cigarettes. A baby certainly should not be given a bone someone else has tasted. Give your baby only fresh, unlicked bones. Toys? Scrape the mud off first, please. Unless it is fresh, untasted mud, of course. Use your discretion. And, as counterintuitive as it may seem, Mother, don't exhale a gust of moist, germy aerated spittle into your baby's crib if you have a cold. Yes, old wives' advice says that coughing on a baby gives it strength, but we now know this is mere superstition. Coughing on a baby during a full moon gives it strength.

7. Unscreened windows and doors.

Because crows can get in. Or swamp miasma. Use modern, germ-proof screens, and boil them once a week.

8. Flies.

This was a great break from previous wisdom, which celebrated the lively role played by "baby's buzzy confederates." You may use a bowie knife to scrape them off, but take care to use the dull edge. Boil the knife first.

9. Dusting or sweeping the room while the baby is in it.

10. Bright sunlight in the baby's eyes, whether awake or asleep.

11. Taking the baby into a home where there is illness.

Point #11 is important to remember, since many young mothers needlessly bring their children along to visit a friend who has taken ill with the Spanish Grippe, or Rheumatic Ague, thinking that the natural health of the baby is contagious. Do not do this! Leave the baby outside when you go into the home where there is illness. If the baby has reached creeping age, weight its gown with lead; it cannot get far.

12. Taking the baby to "movies," or to any other crowded places.

"Movies" are certainly bad, as the anxious, dramatic piano accompaniment can rile up a baby's delicate nerves. Also, the baby may disturb other patrons. Would you go to the theater with your telephone in your pocket, a wire stretching miles behind you, just so that you might receive a call? It is the question that answers itself. And imagine if it should cry while a baby is on the screen! People would conclude that the movies were capable of sound and flee the theater in panic. (See Chapter 7, "Giving Up Your Life," to see how to protect your child in common, everyday trampling situations such as fires, panics, mad horses, etc.)

13. Picking the baby up the minute he cries. Just be sure he is warm and dry; that no pins are sticking him; that hands and feet are not cold. If there is no reason for discomfort let him cry.

Practical parenting in a nutshell: If the child is not being pierced by a sharp metal object, leave him alone. You start picking up babies the moment they cry, they will become so used to having every need met they will be unable to think for themselves, and will be more likely to support socialized pensions or "safety" laws for meatpacking and other patriotic industries.

To review: Clean bones. No flies.

Exercise Is Needed by the Baby

to help him develop properly. He will enjoy a few simple daily exercises and they are better for him than tossing him about or playing roughly with him.

Have the baby on his back for exercises A to C.

Exercise A.
1. Grasp his hands at the sides.
2. Lift them over his head.
3. Bring the bent elbows down to the sides.
4. Straighten elbows and bring hands to the sides.

Repeat four times.

Exercise B.
1. Grasp the foot and bend the knee upward until it touches the abdomen.
2. Straighten the leg.

Repeat four times.

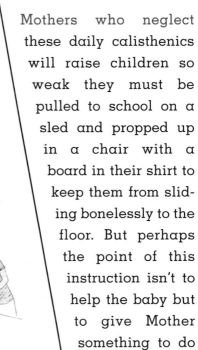

Mothers who neglect these daily calisthenics will raise children so weak they must be pulled to school on a sled and propped up in a chair with a board in their shirt to keep them from sliding bonelessly to the floor. But perhaps the point of this instruction isn't to help the baby but to give Mother something to do besides tossing him about and playing roughly with him.

Apparently, the old-school approach to robustness consisted of pitching the baby across the room and catching him in an apple basket, or tying him to the dog's tail and dropping a squirrel in the room. Many a time did an old country doctor look at a weak infant, peer inquisitively at the mother, and ask: *Is he getting enough tossing? I don't mean throwing him in the air, either. I mean good old-fashioned hurl 'em down the hall tossing. Well, madam? Well?*

Food

Goooood Morning!

Start boiling! Get several gallons going so when the milkman shows up you can pour the entire pot out the window on his head. Filthy, *filthy* man.

CHICAGO'S HEALTH

Care of Baby's Milk

The milk used for the baby should be fresh and the best obtainable. It is better and safer if boiled, even though it is certified or pasteurized milk.

Raw milk makes large, tough curds in the baby's stomach which are hard to digest. Boiled milk gives a fine, soft curd which is easy to digest. Even the calf, for which raw cow's milk is the natural food, cannot digest the curd directly but has to chew it again as a cud. The calf is able to do this but not the baby.

Boiling the milk kills the germs which may be present; this prevents infections of the baby's bowels.

Milk should always be kept cold. It should be placed on ice as soon as received and is best kept in the original bottle until made up for use according to the doctor's formula.

Before removing the cap, the bottle and cap should be cleaned so as to keep dirt out of the milk.

ALWAYS BOIL ME BEFORE FEEDING THE BABY

MILK

This description makes milk sound like more trouble than it's worth, frankly; no avoiding those curds. Raw milk makes for huge, leathery curds that take years to pass, so don't drag Junior out to the barn, prop him under Bossie, aim a teat at his mouth, and let 'er rip. No, use certified milk. Boil it, boil the cap, boil the certificate, submerge the bottle in ammonia, strain the contents through a sieve, then reboil the milk until you have nothing but dried foam, which you may rub into the infant's gums with a washcloth. There. That wasn't all that hard. And my, just look at the time — you've been up for hours. It's already seven A.M.!

Food must be preboiled, then DOUBLE BOILED. And don't worry about what you're boiling — frankly, if you're boiling the food for 45 minutes, it might as well be wood chips or this pamphlet. (Remove the staples.) During the initial boiling phase, make sure you stir the mixture all the time, standing over the stove, ever alert for lump formation. Do not use the boiling time to sit down for the first time today, have a cigarette, and read a magazine about glamorous movie stars laughing in California. You can do that when the child is married — after you have taught her how you stood and boiled farina, that is. The trick is to stir and think of Valentino. Stir slowly. Ohhh, so *slowly*.

Preparing Cereal Food

Oatmeal, farina and other cereals may be used. When prepared for the baby, they should be well cooked.

In preparing this feeding, four ounces of milk should be mixed with four ounces of water and brought to a boil.

The cereal should be added slowly, using one tablespoonful of the heavier cereals like farina, or two of the lighter such as oatmeal.

The mixture should be cooked slowly over an open flame for 15 minutes, stirring all of the time. Sugar (one-half teaspoonful) is to be added and a pinch of salt. The food is now placed in a double boiler and cooked for at least 45 minutes. Enough cereal may be prepared for two days if it can be kept on ice until used. It should always be warmed before it is fed.

A few teaspoonfuls are given the first day, followed by the breast or bottle. More is given each day until by about the tenth day the whole feeding is given, then the breast or bottle may be omitted at this feeding.

Baby can be taught to like a new food

MILK!

**Your closest friend,
your bitterest foe!**

> **Care of Milk.**—Keep milk clean, cold and covered. Milk sours if it is not kept constantly on ice. Milk bottles should always be kept closed and, if possible, in a separate place in the ice-box. Before removing the stopper wash off the bottle (including the top) under the faucet before preparing the food or putting the bottle in the ice-box. You don't know how clean the milkman's hands were when he left the milk. Open milk bottles should not be left standing in the kitchen where they become warm and particles of dust get into them. Milk will easily take up odors. It is very sensitive. It does not need to be sour to be harmful. Milk often reaches a point just before it actually turns sour when it is almost as dangerous as when entirely spoiled.

These instructions are just for milk. Imagine what they had to go through for meat and cheese, to say nothing of opium. The key detail about the milkman's hands gives you a window into the era. Modern milk: You buy it, drink it, recycle the container. Premodern milk: A guy drags the cow to your house, gives Bessie a suppository, wipes his hands on his filthy pants, spits a stream of tobacco juice into his other hand for lubrication, milks the beast right there, and hands you a sloshing pail of Very Sensitive Milk. But what to do with it now that you have it? Simple: Build a milk box, of course.

Home-made Ice-box for Milk.—A cheap ice-box can be made for keeping milk at a proper temperature. Take an ordinary wooden box, and to the cover nail ten thicknesses of newspaper. In the middle of the box place a galvanized pail, and in the center of this pail place a piece of new stove-pipe. A quart bottle of milk can be placed in the stove-pipe, and five cents' worth of ice put around this in the pail. The space between the pail and the sides of the box is filled in with sawdust. When the cover is on, the ice and sawdust will keep the milk in proper condition. This ice-box must be kept clean. Milk should never be kept uncovered, either in an ice-box or anywhere else.

This was before the era of 24-hour convenience stores, of course. Now when you run out of sawdust, you can run down to the gas station and pick up a pound.

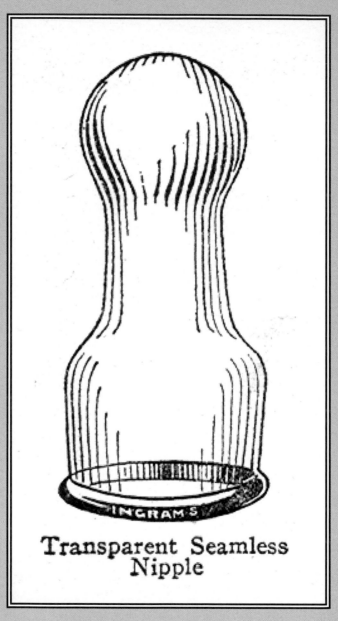

Transparent Seamless
Nipple

Question: NIPPLE OR CONDOM? If it's a nipple, it's just like Mother's! Provided Mother is a she-wolf whose weary teats have been pre-yanked by 16 previous litters, that is.

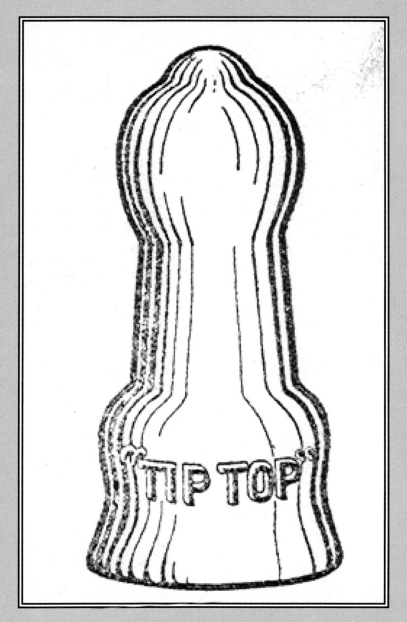

Again, we ask: NIPPLE OR CONDOM? It could be both, of course. It might make a rather small condom that forbade sensation, which would (A) make it a rather poor choice for the marital act, and (B) would serve the brute right.

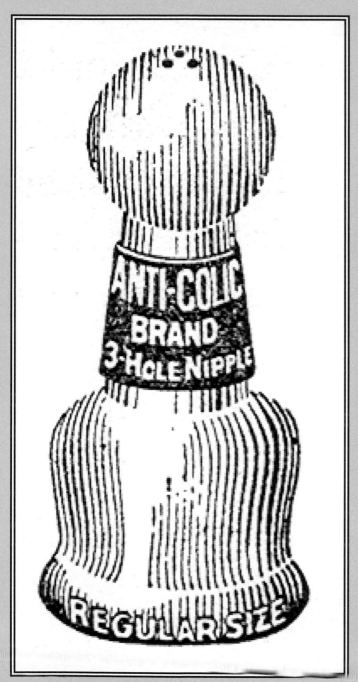

Question: NIPPLE OR SALT-SHAKER? It's a nipple, even though it appears to be a chess piece with a small bowling ball glued on the top. This is an "Anti-Colic Brand 3-Hole Nipple," and you will no doubt note the technical innovation that sets this unit apart: It has holes through which the milk can pass. This invention was credited with a remarkable reduction in the infant mortality rate.

By "Anti-Colic," of course, they meant "incredible bouts of colic that peeled the wallpaper and made the barnyard animals shift uneasily in their pens, several hundred feet away." See also "Painless Dentistry."

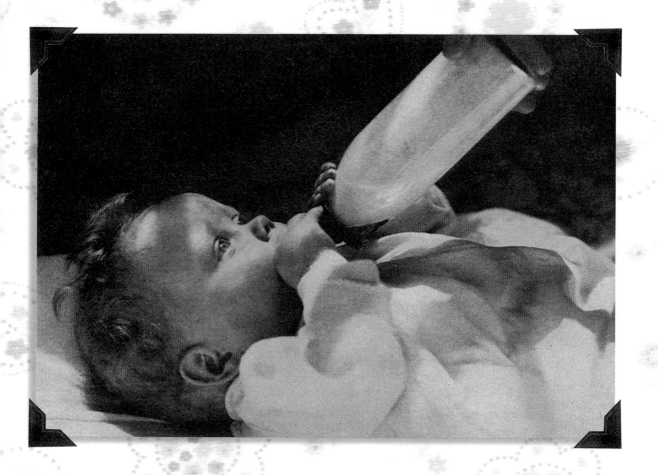

In many of the old illustrations from the 1940s, the milk glows in such an incandescent fashion that you expect the article to tout the nutritious power of radium. But they had to give it all a wondrous glow. They had to give it that lovely holy buff. Why? Because the actual mechanics of feeding the tyke involved a logistical nightmare that made D-Day look like a hop over a puddle to deliver a May basket.

The following article from 1943 elaborates on the procedure in excruciating detail, and any modern parent will regard it with great gratitude for three modern inventions: powdered formula, the microwave, and birth-control pills.

Wash in hot soapy water and rinse thoroughly in clear hot water the following articles, then place them in the sterilizing kettle: the large pitcher or jar, the measuring cup, both of the nipple jars and lids, rubber caps, glass nipple caps, the nipples, the four measuring spoons, the mixing spoon, the silver knife, the can opener, the cup, and the tongs. Examine the holes in the nipples to make sure they are not clogged. A good way to test them is to fill each nipple with water, insert the left forefinger, and squeeze the tip of the nipple between the forefinger and thumb of the right hand. A stream of water will be forced through each hole that is clear.

Everything in the sterilizing kettle should be completely submerged, but if you find that the kettle doesn't hold sufficient water to completely cover the pitcher and jars, turn them upside down, cover closely, and the live steam will sterilize them. Time the sterilizing for five full minutes from the moment the water is actively boiling.

Meanwhile, wash seven bottles (*Turn to page* 50)

. . . and then put the bottles upside down on a mat woven from grass you collected this morning when you were out in the field selecting beets for lunch, then take the kettle off the stove. Meanwhile, mash the beets in a pan with your feet, taking care to remove the dirt first; if the dirt has not been removed, sterilize the beets, set them on fire, mix the ash with rubbing alcohol, and pour on the ground. Examine the holes in your nipples. Notice how you can do that? How you can actually pick them up and stare your nipples straight in the eye? Couldn't do that before you had a kid. Now, while you're boiling the pots you will use for boiling small items, get out the grinding wheel and hone that six-inch dowel down into a pin for diapers.

Understand that we have not yet begun to make the formula. If your child was hungry when you began, it's a flyblown skeleton by the time you finish making the formula.

It's Easy to Fix a Formula

There's no mystery about this important item. Whether you use fresh, dried, or evaporated milk, preparing Baby's main meal at this stage is simple as can be

1 The irradiated evaporated milk formula is easiest of all to prepare. Here are the things you'll need: can of milk; Karo, or whatever sweetening your doctor advises; as much boiled water as your formula calls for; glass measuring pitcher; mixing pitcher; measuring spoon; sieve; funnel; sterilized nursing bottles; sterile cotton for bottle stoppers

It's easy to fix a formula? Says you, buster. Oddly enough, this illustration would appear years later in the *Anarchist's Cookbook*; apparently you can make one hell of an incendiary device using just these same materials. (Assuming the bottle of clear liquid is kerosene, that is.) The roll of cotton is used to ignite the bomb or purify the milk, depending on how you feel about the current administration.

FIG. 167. Formula and feeding equipment: 1. Sterilizer and bottle rack. 2. Double boiler with capacity indication marks. 3. Graduate—may be enamel or pyrex. 4. Tray containing the following: 5. Nipple jar with perforated cover. 6. Plain lid for nipple jar. 7. Bottle for the day's supply of drinking water for the baby. 8. Seven 8-oz. bottles. 9. One 4-oz. bottle (for water or orange juice). 10. Funnel with removable strainer. 11. Jar with cover (for used nipples). 12. Steri-seal cap (nipple protector). 13. Jar of sugar (if used in formula). 14. Small graduate or jar to hold forceps, spoons, etc., after sterilized and while preparing formula. 15. Forceps. 16. Measuring spoons. 17. Wooden spoon (for stirring formula while cooking and cooling). 18. Orange juicer. 19. Knife (for orange). 20. Stirring rod or leveler (useful in turning nipples). 21. Can opener (if canned milk is used). 22. Babeads for cleaning bottles (instead of brush). 23. Nipple brush. 25. Bottle brush (if Babeads are not used). 25. Clean tea towels. 26. Hot water plate (when foods are added to the diet). 27. Food masher (used in preparing first foods).

Sweet Judas on a stick! Are we feeding a baby or taking out its kidneys?

Next time you hear a modern parent complain about how hard it is to get little Cypheria to eat her organic paella, show them this ad from 1944. Yes, food shortages. Not a shortage of Life-Size My Little Pony dolls or a shortage of those darling jumpers from DKNY with the sequined straps, but a shortage of food. Puts things in perspective, no? Explains why Mom or Dad got cranky when you took one bite of your succulent pork chop and pushed away your plate because you'd eaten a bag of Fritos. They didn't fight in World War II so you could eat when and what you pleased. Well — actually, yes, they did, but that's not the point. Eat your pork chop.

A GOOD IDEA

nutritionally, gastronomically!

Emergency Steak

. . . extending meat with WHEATIES... These whole wheat flakes (whole grain) help to supplement meat's food values. And Wheaties add a rich nut-like flavor.

* * *

Emergency Steak. Delicious! Try this meat-extender recipe tested by the famous Betty Crocker staff.

WHEATIES
"Breakfast of Champions"

Mom, what's for dinner?

Emergency Steak.

What's that?

Chopped butt flank extended with breakfast cereal.

You said butt!

You're right, sweetie. I meant chopped heinie steak loaded up with Wheaties and char-seared until it looks like it was dug up from a Dresden cemetery. Here you go.

Yum! Can we have Crisis Pancakes for breakfast?

Of course we can. Don't we always?

Light up the soup...
it's a birthday party!

You know how this goes. Mom leans back, sways, lights a Lark with the last match, then looks at the silent and crestfallen kids around the table. "Well? Whaddya think?" she says, slurring her words a bit. "I sawit inna magazine. Thought it was cute."

"Mom, it's soup," says the birthday boy. "It's tomato soup. I thought we were going to have hot dogs."

"Ahh, think of it as ketchup drink. 'S got rice. You like rice. Ev'body blow it out! Counta three! One, two, three."

The kids blow on the candles, which tip into the liquid and hiss, spilling wax into the soup. The air has that blown-out-candle stink that always promises cake and ice cream.

But there is no cake or ice cream in sight.

when you think of the Circus...

...you think of fun

when you think of *energy*...

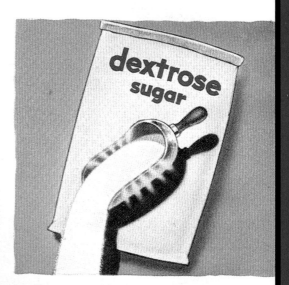

...think of dextrose sugar

Painted horse-impersonators are fun and full of energy: Therefore, you should consume great scoops of sugar. Hard to argue with the logic.

This 1945 ad from a sugar-producing consortium reassured moms that sugar is a wondrous, natural miracle for which every cell of your body cries out in joy. Or, as your kid puts it: *More Frosted Chocolate Sugar Puffs, please! Hurry, Ma, I'm comin' down! Don't make me pawn your jewelry for a roll of NECCO Wafers again!*

The ad comes from the tail end of the war, when ads were reduced to telling you all the things you would have once that bastard Hitler was dead, so the copy notes that demand for sugar exceeds capacity. Apparently, it was all going to make candy bars to give to French hookers. But don't worry — more sugar will soon hit the market and sate the jones of your twitchy little kid. In the meantime, go lick a clown.

Lunchtime quandaries! What to serve—reliable brine-packed wieners, endorsed by the product of hillbilly-holler inbred marriages, or liver spread?

Then again, you can't go wrong with gravy-draped pig cerebellums, can you?

But only if you're out of ox tongue. It's packed in agar agar jelly! Remember: severed ruminant tongue. Kids ask for it by name.

Not a fan of ox tongue? How about good old dependable lunch tongue?

Bowels

The Golden Age of Constipation

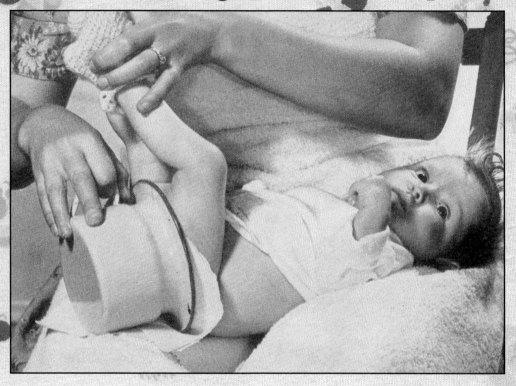

Every new parent confronts the curious palette of infant poop; every new caregiver wonders anew why we feed them corn, since it seems to pass through their small bodies with the ease of a criminal with a diplomatic passport. These things are timeless. But the concern over constipation seems to have abated somewhat. It certainly couldn't get any worse. Judging from the following examples from our golden past, most of America's youth was incapable of producing anything more than a hard half-inch stool per fiscal year.

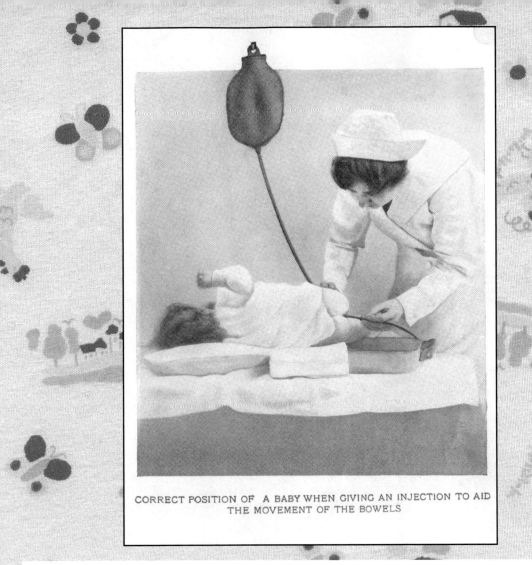

CORRECT POSITION OF A BABY WHEN GIVING AN INJECTION TO AID
THE MOVEMENT OF THE BOWELS

"Correct," in this case, meaning the child should turn aside in shame and raise a hand in feeble protest over the insertion of a hard rubber hose up its tender chute. The observant reader will no doubt notice that the bag is suspended in air; either the background has been removed somehow, or the nurse's assistant was actually a vampire and hence incapable of being photographed. It would certainly explain the baby's posture; the glint of those hungry, pointed canines would stir all manner of ancestral fears.

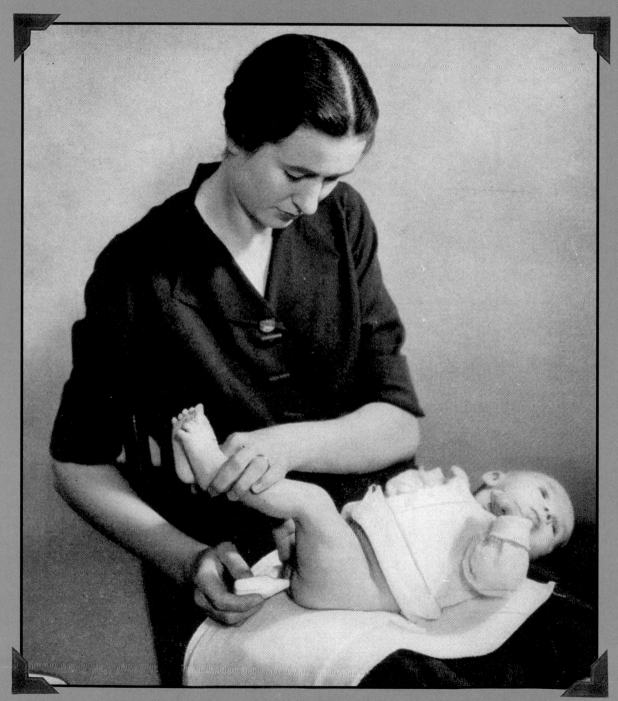

This appears to be one of the few times in life one can be this disinterested in such a situation.

Any idea what's going on here? Why, it's simple: The baby is being oiled to keep its joints limber and supple. Frequently, babies would seize up, painfully, and emit a series of rusted squeaks. Galvanized diapers solved the problem for most, but general lubrication was still prescribed into the 1930s.

Actually, the baby's getting some soap up the keister to hasten the end of a costive fit, and it seems to have induced a rather contemplative state. The child would be less sanguine if he could read the caption to this illustration, which cautions that "the suppository should not be completely inserted." If Mother has to be told not to shove the entire brick of Ivory up Junior's hindquarters, constipation is the least of his problems.

Training the Baby to the Toilet

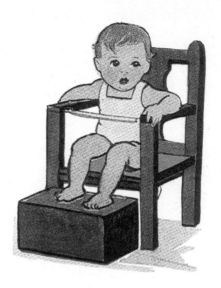

The baby should by this time be well trained in using the pot. A small extra seat which fits over the ordinary toilet may be purchased or a small toilet chair placed over the pot. A foot-rest should be provided. On such a seat the baby is fastened so that he cannot fall out and he may then be safely left alone for five to ten minutes. It is best not to give him anything to play with at such times. He should understand that he is there for a definite purpose.

The mother may teach baby to say a simple word such as "chair-chair" when he feels the desire to pass water or have a bowel movement. She may say the words when placing him on the seat. He will soon learn to tell her when he needs the toilet.

He should be placed on the seat on arising, after eating, at regular times during the day, and just before going to bed.

The President of the School of Sanitary Instruction will be glad to have mothers write to him concerning their baby problems.

Any Word from the Governor, Warden?

Thus were babies trained in the 1920s: First, they obliquely refer to the "chair-chair." Granted, it beats "crapper-crapper" or "pot o' gold" or any other euphemism, but somehow it seems unwise to make a chair synonymous with a mechanism for collecting bodily waste, lest the kid grow up squatting on a rocker like a chimp. You could say "toilet-toilet," so the kid learns to narrow it down somewhat. The word "bathroom" has also been approved by experts who assure us that no one goes to hell for saying the word, even though certain unmentionable organs are exposed to air and light in these chambers.

Note that the child is supposed to be left alone for ten minutes so he can associate the chair-chair with abandonment and punishment. Flash-forward thirty years to the psychiatrist's office: I believe your constipation is all in your head. So to speak.

BEAT THE CRAP OUT OF 'EM
Ads from the Golden Age of Corporal Punishment

Here we have a long, long series of ads that ran in parenting magazines. Same scenario, same horrors, same happy ending. Typical:

"I don't _ever_ want to go home again!"

Why, sweetie? *Because Mommy uses harsh caustic laxatives that make me feel like I'm trying to pass a handful of thumbtacks, that's why! And she beats me if I don't take it!* The mother is soon set on the right path, introduced to modern nonsearing laxatives, and the child agrees to go home. The text notes that Mom had spanked the child to get her to take the laxative, which strikes contemporary eyes as cruel and ridiculous. Which it was, but remember: We're talking about a time when it wasn't just permissible to beat your child or beat your dog, you could actually use your dog to beat your child.

More examples from this lovely ad campaign follow.

"If he spanks me, I'm gonna run away from home!"

Same problem; child doesn't want to drink a teaspoon of drain unblocker, so Dad opts for the dependable old-fashioned method of Hairbrush Persuasion. Ah, the good old days: When a man could come home from work and expect his children to have already moved their bowels — and if they hadn't, he could follow them into the street and thrash them with a grooming tool, perhaps as a lesson to all those Little Tommy Tight-Guts up and down the block. Y'all better crap now, or you're next! Hear?

"This is the last time he spanks that boy!"

A young mother and dad both learn something about safe child care

You know, a mother just knows things. Sometimes she'll hand the brush to her husband, shrug, head up the stairs — and stop. And think: Really, is beating him with a grooming implement the best way to coax compacted waste from his tiny body?

Maybe Tommy is so reasonable all the time because he lives in absolute terror of Big Tom? Just a thought. I mean, look at Big Tom: the picture of compassion. Let me comfort you, O my child. On second thought, there's still some lacquer left on the brush. Saddle up.

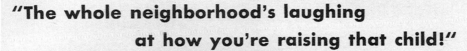

"The whole neighborhood's laughing at how you're raising that child!"

It wasn't always about making innocent bottoms as red as an autumn bonfire; sometimes the problem of the Wrong Laxative manifested itself as a collective form of peer humiliation. Here we have the older sister informing her younger sis just how the neighborhood regards her parenting skills. "Sis," I said, "come down to earth about young Ted. You're going to spoil him with all this 'special business.' Special toys, special soap, special powder . . . even a special laxative."

The proper response would be to tell the neighborhood to withdraw its bony nose from her business and go worry about Mr. Andrews, who hangs around the soda fountain and buys drinks for all the kids if they sit on his lap. But no, he's a retired judge and a Mason and plays Santa every year, so no one thinks twice. You're all a bunch of small-minded fools, and I rue the day Big Ted brought us back to this place! My God, you all make Gopher Prairie look like the boulevards of Paris! Oh, I'm sorry, sis, you didn't read that book, did you? No, if you can't see Gene Tierney playing the heroine in the movie, you won't touch a book unless it's sitting on top of your copy of *Modern Movie*. Well, I won't apologize! He got horrible hives from that soap you gave me, and it made his hair come away in clumps! Am I to be ridiculed because I sent away for something that didn't have quite so much lye in it? Sick! You all make me horribly, horribly sick!

But no. She conforms. She knows the price if she doesn't. How do you think her sister got wise to the neighborhood's opinion, anyway? The druggist talks. The grocer talks. You could send away for something, but the mailman talks. Oh, they're nice enough people; they always smile, wish you a good day, tip their hats. Inevitably: *How's young Ted?* At first it was delightful — to have everyone so interested in your child's welfare. How unlike Manhattan, where they were just as likely to push a carriage aside to make the train. But after a while it began to seem, well, oh I don't *know*, I'm sure I'm making too much about this, but — well, sis, it seems like they think the baby's *theirs*, somehow, like they all have a stake in it. Am I crazy? Oh, sometimes I think I will just go mad cooped up here in this house, with Ted on the road so much. I'm so grateful you came over. So very grateful. I've missed you *terribly* since our row about the food. Young Ted has really taken to the brand you suggested. He loves it! The little devil on the box makes him laugh so. And to think I was feeding him that stuff with the silly old Quaker on the box!

What's that? Not more medicine. Please, sis. I'm already so tired, and it makes me so *very* weak. I know you say that's normal at first, but when will I start to feel like myself again?

Oh, not a *laxative*. Oh, does it have to be a laxative again?

What do you mean everyone in Polanski, Ohio, goes at the same time? What can you possibly mean?

"Bill Todd—how **can** you spank that child on Christmas!"

A young father learns how to settle one child problem the easy way!

Then it's back to business as usual. Here we have a charming holiday tale in which Mom raises a perfectly good question. And Bill answers, sensibly, "Oh, it's easy! I just put my shoe in my right hand, like this. And what the hell is that on your head?"

Needless to say, young Bill is soon irrigated with laxatives he likes to drink, and the holiday house echoes with percussive detonations from Christmas morn 'til New Year's Eve.

One has to ask: Hairbrushes? Shoes? Did the average father prepare to paddle his child with the palm of his hand, and think: *No, it's not hard enough?*

Eventually, spanking children because they refused to take foul-tasting bowel-blasters on command ceased to be the national vogue. Castor oil was out; beating them was out. The Future of Constipation Relief was at hand.

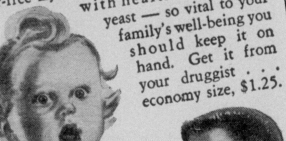

Zymenol!

Now with more Zyme! This product may be for the entire family, and keep everybody trotting to the pot at intervals so regular, City Hall calls to see if they can set the tower clock by your collective noon evacuation, but: It has different effects on different ages. For babies, it produces a stunned sense of dull amazement, or perhaps bewitching hallucinations; hard to tell. Young men are overcome by the desire to quit the varsity squad and join the Poetry Club, so they may learn to express the wondrous emotions Zymenol has bestowed.

No sonnets, books, or manuals
yet sing of tasty granules
So this gay toast I do propose
to Zymenol and Zymelose.
I sing of costive bouts most wrenching!
Of food-stopp'd colons now unclenching!
I shout —

Very nice, Robert. Thank you.
There's more!
Thank you, Robert.

Overnight, Freddy went from THIS...

to THIS thanks to Phillips'!

Gentle, effective Milk of Magnesia gives <u>better</u> relief— more <u>complete</u> relief—than single-purpose laxatives!

Constipation, the high jumper's worst enemy. Message: It's amazing how much higher you can jump when you're six pounds lighter.

Fatherhood

WHEN FATHER KNEW *Best*

The fifties, we're told, was the time when the wise and steady hand of the patriarch could settle all disputes, fix all broken toys, set bones, and come up with a cure for both polio and Communism if you just let him sit in his favorite chair and think about things.

Well, no. Dip into the material aimed at mothers — that is, the people who were dealing with the kids on a molecular level — and you see an entirely different view of the dad. He's a clue-deprived brute at worst, a gentle buffoon at best, someone who would fill the baby bottle with Schlitz and wrap the baby in a newspaper diaper if you didn't keep an eye on him.

Sure, he's part of the family. In the sense that Pluto is part of the solar system.

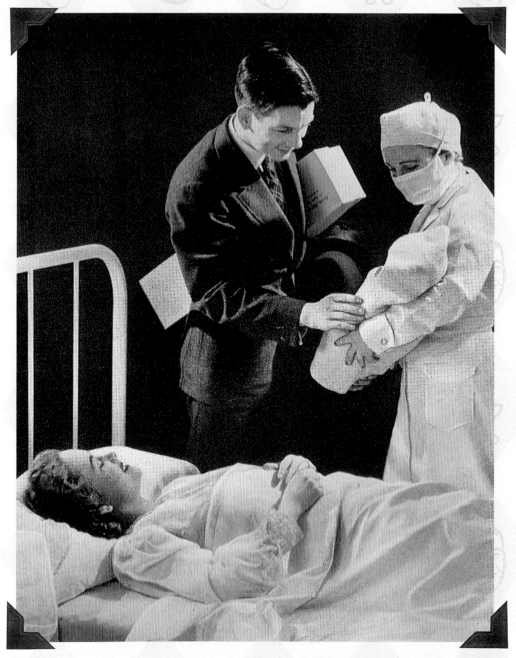

Congratulations, sir — you're the proud father of a fire extinguisher!

Mundugamor fathers have always guarded adolescent girls,
spear in hand, lest they slip out for midnight rendezvous

From 1942, a story about old and new styles of dad behavior. Old and busted: sitting up all night with a weapon guarding half-naked jailbait. What's he thinking? *Those new grass skirts — they show too much leg.* And who is the spear intended for? Any dad can sympathize with the desire to run through some greasy Romeo who's come to break his princess's heart, but the caption makes it sound as if Daddy's Little Girl gets six feet of spear through the rib cage if she steals off the porch.

Modern man need not resort to such savagery; here a modern father — who is wearing 47 pounds of wool, incidentally — puts down his newspaper — which is two yards wide, incidentally — and enters Lawgiver Mode to reassure his daughter. No, my dear, a lobotomy is nothing to fear. It brings peace. Peace and calm. Why, look at your mother.

How good a
FAMILY MAN
is your husband?

You can, if you wish, spend the better part of a year at the Library of Congress, paging through every issue of every 1952 magazine aimed at men, from *Argosy* to *Zebra Wrangler Quarterly*, and you will never see a story titled "How Good a Family Woman Is Your Wife?" The subject was never conceived, let alone broached.

Look at this poor bastard. *Look* at him. For starters, he's improperly scaled for the illustration; he looks to be about 97 feet tall here, some sort of giant she bagged with that gun she keeps concealed in her huge skirt.

The hat is an afterthought, jammed on his head as some sort of brain-dampening device — good Lord, you can see it in his dead eyes, his slack and soon-to-drool mouth. He's probably barely able to put two words together, but somewhere in the back of his brain a thought stirs and struggles to be heard: *I used to fish, once. I had a life of my own.*

But then she stares extra hard and smiles, and his head is full of that sound you hear when you tune the radio to the place where there ain't no station. He knows that sound. He supposes that's the way it is for everyone. *Po-ker? Is that a word? How come some-times when she turns away and the static goes down I hear the word poker an' I think about girls? Purty ones in underwear?*

BEFORE YOU CRITICIZE YOUR HUSBAND AS A FATHER

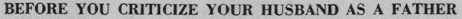

ASK YOURSELF THESE SEARCHING QUESTIONS

DO YOU *feel you must always keep the children from "bothering" their father?*

DO YOU *usually refer to the children as "my son" and "my daughter"?*

DO YOU *belittle your husband before the children?*

DO YOU *threaten your children with "just wait until your father gets home"?*

DO YOU *confide things to the children which they are not supposed to tell their father?*

DO YOU *always stand between the children and your husband when he tries to discipline them?*

DO YOU *tend to be "all mother" and not enough wife?*

BEFORE YOU CRITICIZE YOUR HUSBAND AS A FATHER

ASK YOURSELF THESE SEARCHING QUESTIONS

And *then* you can carve him up however you please. Let's answer those questions, shall we?

DO YOU *feel you must always keep the children from "bothering" their father?*

"Bothering" can mean many things, from "breathing in a room where he is reading the newspaper" to "curling up in his lap and giving him an expression of love which equals, if not temporarily surpasses, that which you have received."

DO YOU *usually refer to the children as "my son" and "my daughter"?*

And if so, is it because this man is actually a drifter your husband hired to paint the shed? He seemed to offer so much promise and excitement when you first saw him sweating in the noon heat with his shirt off. You invited him inside for a beer, which was the decent thing to do — but then he grabbed you in the pantry, and you felt alive, alive for the first time in so long. Of course, your husband was suspicious — you were too neat to let spilled flour stay unswept for a day, and why were you so flushed, and what were these white handprints doing everywhere — and that's when the handyman hit him, hit him hard, with a sound you'll never forget no matter how hard you try, but in that horrible moment you knew you loved him, you'd do anything, including faking the accident with the car. What did you feel as it plunged down the ravine, if not a glorious, delirious sense of freedom coupled with an almost delicious awareness of your own damnation? Is that it?

No? Okay, never mind.

DO YOU *belittle your husband before the children?*

This is wrong. Always belittle the children first. Then the husband.

DO YOU *threaten your children with "just wait until your father gets home"?*

If you do, and Father is away in Korea and unlikely to return until the Chinese resistance is mopped up and the UN declares a truce — which seems damned unlikely, given the pace of recent talks — then use a notebook to keep track of all the sins for which father will have to levy punishment. Be aware that he may be disinclined to do so, and could add "I've seen a hundred good men die to take a hill we abandoned the next morning, honey. I'm not going to spank Junior because he told Mrs. Johnson she had a wrinkly neck. Hell, if he says it again, I'll raise his allowance. He's right. And I've seen too much death to pretend otherwise. Junior! Boy! Come here. We're going over to Mrs. Johnson's house right now and tell her a thing or two. I don't care if I've been drinking! You'd drink, too, if you saw a man try to stuff his guts back in his skin after a shell ripped him open!"

Again with the gut-stuffing. He brought that up yesterday as a reason he couldn't oil the screen door.

DO YOU *confide things to the children which they are not supposed to tell their father?*

If so, your acidic diatribes about "male misconceptions about vaginal orgasms" may be going right over their heads.

DO YOU *always stand between the children and your husband when he tries to discipline them?*

If so, and you're trying to get in on the spanking, well, for heaven's sake just ask.

DO YOU *tend to be "all mother" and not enough wife?*

And don't give us the "why-whatever-do-you-mean" look here, sister; you know exactly what we're talking about. Coming to bed in a quilted nightgown that looks like something a firefighter would wear, your legs as stubbly as a brush for combing nits from a horse's mane, a pound of cold cream on your face, your hair up in curlers beneath a crinkly plastic bag. What did you do the other night — you came to bed with a big fish, and said, "Not tonight. I have a haddock."

And when he looked confused you made him wear the hat. He complains at first, but the hat always solves *that* problem.

Hi! I'm your Dad! Would someone look at me, please?

Anyone?

Hey, Junior — *you'll* look at me! Aw, take your eyes off Mom for a moment. Get used to it; she's going to be doting on that little one for months. Way of the world, son. But you can count on me! Son? Son?

Hey, little punkin — surely your old pop is more interesting than that heap of mashed squash Mom's prepared, isn't it? I can pretend I'm mashed squash! I can make burping noises like I've eaten a lot of mashed squash! Later, I can give you a pony ride to Happy Squash Land! Don't cry — please, she always takes you away into the next room and gives me that look when I say something and you cry. She says you're sensitive to people's voices. Well, so am I. Which is why I'd like to hear one someday, particularly if it called my frickin' name.

Hey! Hello! I've been home for an hour! Anyone care how my day went? Where's my pipe and slippers? Do I have to get a dog? I don't care if he humps my leg; any attention at this point would be just great. Or should I just grow breasts? That do it? Okay, then.

Anyone asks, I'll be at the tavern. Oh, don't everyone try to stop me at once!

(*slam*)

SO YOU'RE GOING TO BE A FATHER

It's a wise father who shares
in getting ready for the baby
and takes an active part
in his—or her—care.
Here are a few things
to do before the baby comes

From the mid-fifties, this is an interesting series of photos, most of which feature this guy who appears to be on the lam from the authorities, perhaps on a charge of impersonating Tony Curtis, and finds himself confronting the confusing details of fatherhood.

Here, for example, he's scraping off a deep wicker basket, perhaps in preparation for putting the baby in the reeds to save him from the Pharaoh. Let's examine the rest of the delightful tableaus!

Before you find a doctor, invest in a good reporter's notebook. Don't sit; this is important. Stand in the back and ask questions. Identify yourself as "Joe Father" from *The New Dad Times-Gleaner* or some such fun journal. You might wonder: How do I know if he's a real doctor? Simple: Real doctors put their stethoscopes right on the

As soon as your wife is pretty sure she's going to have a baby, go with her to see a doctor. Together, choose the doctor carefully—if possible, an obstetrician. Write down his instructions, settle on his fee, find out about hospital costs. Ask about the hospital; a good one has a certificate of approval from the American College of Surgeons.

desk, like this one, and they always push the ashtray over to the mother, because they know it can be strenuous on pregnant women to reach too far to tap an ash.

If possible, get an obstetrician, but hell, any sort of M.D. will do. Proctologists will do in a pinch; they may not know the city, but they know the state, if you get our drift. "Settle on his fee" — by which we mean dicker. If his price is too high at first, say something like "Hey, Doc, do you throw in whitewalls too? I mean, come on. What are we paying you for? We're paying you not to drop it, is what. But I understand you got your overhead. Toss in the circumcision for free and we got a deal." Or something like that, just to show you're not to be pushed around.

This would also be a good time to hit him up for some Benzedrine. What's the worst he can say?

P lan for those evenings when you *will* have to stay home. After Junior arrives, you'll have a chance to pursue a hobby. What would you enjoy doing when you're baby-sitting? Taking up photography in a big way, maybe; or making things in a home workshop—unless, of course, you're one of those men who prefer a game of chess or relaxing with a good book.

Note to the tone: *You will have to stay home.* Welcome to the world in which even the magazines on the coffee table have the same tone of voice as your wife, pal.

"Unless, of course, you're one of those men who prefer a game of chess or relaxing with a good book." But of course you're *not* one of those men, are you? Look at you! Everything about you screams PAROLE. So photography it is! No more skulking out in your makeshift darkroom in the potting shed —— now you have time to develop the film while the kid's sleeping and the wife's at her mom's. No, you can pursue your dreams, and finally install that camera in the women's bathroom by the office down at the plant.

No longer does a pregnant woman retire into a shapeless garment and practically go into seclusion. Have friends in for the evening. Go out to the movies, to parties, picnics; before long you'll be home-bound much of the time. Your wife needs to take things in moderation, but there's no reason to forego your usual fun just because you're "expecting."

And what could be more fun than taking a 1 A.M. walk in a suit coat down that trench your neighbor dug by his picket fence? Make sure to hold your hat awkwardly so that it both symbolizes your emasculation and suggests a vaginal contour, as though you too were about to give birth. In a way, you know, you are because —

Wait a minute — that's not you. What happened? Who is this fellow? He's cutting in on your time, is he? Taking your wife out to a midnight picnic while you're pulling an extra shift so you can pay for the baby. Well, so you can change the film in the camera. But the bonus money will come in handy when it's time to buy the crib. Or maybe buy some knuckle-dusters to deal with this guy. He's got some nerve.

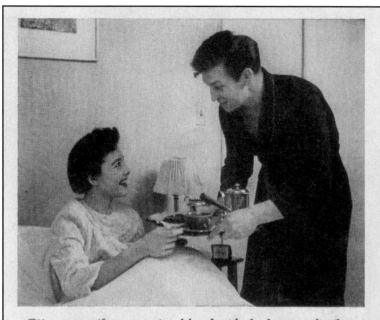

Give your wife an occasional hand with the housework—always a welcome gesture, but especially now when she may tire more easily. Serving her Sunday breakfast in bed will meet with tremendous appreciation—if she likes breakfast in bed. Be extra understanding and thoughtful at this time when she may be under emotional as well as physical strains.

And if she doesn't like breakfast in bed, well, what's wrong with her? Don't all dames like breakfast in bed? It's classy. It's what they do in the movies. Look, you got toast here. You got coffee. Okay, Sanka — I couldn't figure out the percolator. You got an egg and a candle and a match, so you can cook up an omelette or whatever. Look, I gotta go.

What? What do you mean, I don't want you to come to the kitchen? Don't be ridiculous. I wanted to give you breakfast in bed, that's all. No, you don't hear anyone else in the kitchen. It's the radio. It's playing some soap opera. Yes, on a Saturday morning. You want me to bring her in here so you can hear it? Okay, then.

What? I said *do you want me to bring it in here.* Bring *her* in here? I didn't say anything of the sort — aw, you're nuts. Look, I gotta go. I got something on the stove.

No, it ain't Muriel. Jeezis, Mary, do all pregnant women go nuts? Here. Here's a cigarette. Stop *cryin'*, already.

Okay, she says she's havin' pains, but look at her. Does she look pregnant? Has she ever really looked pregnant? And who takes the time to do her eyebrows before she goes to the doctor at 3 A.M?

Are you sure that was the doctor she called? What if Gaspipe Harry's waiting in the parking lot outside the hospital? What

Photographs by Giles

Off for the blessed event! For weeks your wife's had her bag packed. Beside the telephone you've placed the names and telephone numbers of the doctor (office and home) and the hospital. You've been making sure to have plenty of gas in the car. You've learned the fastest route to the hospital and which entrance is open at three in the morning.

if it's that square-john with the tie clasp who took her for a stroll the other night? Nah — he's in no shape to answer the phone, not unless he's learned to pick it up with his feet.

Ahh, look at her. She's scared. Really scared. Not like Kansas City, either: Maybe she's on the level. Say something nice.

Uh, hon?

"Yeah, Joe?"

It had better be a boy.

What? WHA'D I SAY?

113

Playtime with Daddy

HERE ARE IDEAS FOR A HAPPY TIME YOUR CHILDREN WILL ALWAYS REMEMBER AND CHERISH

Well, OK, if you want him to remember his childhood as one long acid trip. Imagine the therapy sessions:

"I remember Daddy was holding the leg of a big moon-headed clown man. I tried to reach the fish, but Mommy always put it just out of my reach and then she'd laugh and then the horrible African mask, the one I told you about? The one that always changed to show what I was really feeling? It would look really fearful and nervous. The worst part was that Daddy seemed to think he was hiding but he really wasn't. No, the worst part was his shoes."

"I see. And what do you think this represents?"

"I think it represents the fact that they were both art directors for a magazine devoted to half-assed ideas about what kids want, is what I think. I'm not making this up. That man-thing went up in the attic after a while, and it wasn't until high school that I had the nerve to look at him. It was lying on a box, the one I told you about? With all the magazines about oily weight-lifters."

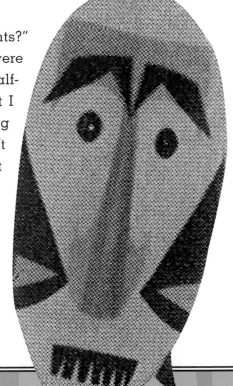

If fathers weren't clueless or absent, they were . . .

UNNERVING

Jes' between you and me, offerin' their tender souls to Satan is my favoritest part of bein' a dad. For some it's watchin' them grow, teachin' them the ways of the world — for me it's the power I get here on earth by sending my dark lord a steady supply of innocent spirits. This makes three so far! I'm *sure* to get that promotion now.

I wish my deal hadn't sucked the life outta the wife — she looks like my ma, frankly — but them's the breaks.

MODERN DAD

The new father pulls out his pocket in the universal gesture of the freshly impoverished. No more fun for you, fella; no more wide-screen 14-inch TVs in your future. It's rental clubs and fuzzy pictures until Junior graduates.

This is from 1962, and demonstrates that era's conception of the young new dad: thinning hair (all that fallout), a bow tie cinched tight (the sixties as we understand them had not yet begun; by '71 he would be wearing an ascot and muttonchops), and a pipe. This still was the acceptable form of tobacco consumption for fathers, and implied seriousness and domesticity. Cigar men ran businesses and boxing rings; cigarette men were spies at the gaming tables of Monte Carlo. Pipe men stayed home and puffed, reading the paper, patting the spaniel on the head, thinking about world affairs, gravely evaluating the effects the Negro Problem would have on the nation, and wishing he could rub the bowl of the pipe and turn into Hugh Hefner. SOB got all the trim.

New Sixties Dad is having trouble adjusting, but this booklet helps him realize two important facts: The child comes first, and his life is over.

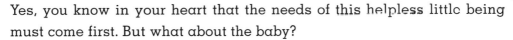

Yes, you know in your heart that the needs of this helpless little being must come first. But what about the baby?

Most fathers look to their families for most of life's chief satisfactions, for their sense of pride, achievement and self-respect. Their work is often not quite interesting or challenging enough to depend on for most of these. Children provide much of the reason for this commitment to family life.

As a new father, you feel you are an understanding husband, able to accept your wife's giving the bulk of her attention to the baby. You know the needs of this helpless little being come first because his wants can be put off only for a little while.

Dad seems to be unable to form the proper gesture here; his brain is firing different messages. Signal for another drink! No. Grab on to the strap on the train that takes you home, or, as you call it these days, the Ignoratorium! No. Hail a cab for the airport to catch a flight to Mexico! No. Wave silently in a futile bid for attention before she realizes the door's open and asks if you want the baby to catch a cold.

Yes, *that's* the one.

I'll nurture, dammit, but I'm not happy about it. I'll wear this emasculating symbol of domestic imprisonment, but I'll radiate short, blunt lines from my head to indicate my displeasure.

And look at this: I can pinch an inch on my waist now. Oh, great. Like I really want to start wearing that girdle again.

Yet whatever your level of income, unless you are in a very high bracket, you sometimes feel that you are not giving your wife and children everything you should. This can bring feelings of frustration and failure. For some men who let these feelings build up, resentment and

anger are eventually directed toward the family as the source of demands impossible to fulfill. And sometimes a man feels great disappointment because he thinks he is not providing his family enough. He may even begin to lose self-esteem and confidence in his ability to cope with the world outside the family.

Everyone smile as Daddy blows out his back to shove the cornucopia into the living room so it may vomit forth consumer goods!

This is the low point in Modern Dad's life, right here. Surely it gets better; it cannot get worse.

Nope. Junior grows up and shreds the contracts the boss needs this morning. At least his adorable high-jinks take Dad's mind off more worrisome matters, like the fact that his wife has become a blow-up sex doll doing an impersonation of Munch's *The Scream*.

But! Salvation comes in the form of modern tranquilizers. The doctor explains the features and benefits of modern pharmaceutical palliatives — and the best part is that not only do they go well with highballs, the effect is doubled. Dad has a question: "Will I stay up late at night boring holes in the ceiling with my sleepless eyes as I contemplate the indisputable fact that this child is the manifestation of my own mortality?"

"Certainly not," the doctor chuckles, erasing a few words on the prescription and doubling the dosage. "You'll sleep like a baby."

"Meaning, attached to my wife's breast?" Dad says. " 'Cause that would be something new."

And now all is well. Dad is tanked out so hard he doesn't notice the newspaper is just a blank sheet of paper. He doesn't hear the clatter of knitting needles that invariably precedes the announcement of pregnancy.

He doesn't even notice that his son has not grown an inch yet he somehow has a five-year-old daughter.

All he knows is that he doesn't dream about the cornucopia anymore. Those dreams were bad toward the end. The thing had *teeth*.

Secrets of a

Pin-Up Girl...

She'll stand queer maneuvers with safety pins—on one condition. That's if those funny people, her parents, will pay attention to the most important thing!

She *must* have her Carnation!

She's got an inexperienced little inside that begs for Carnation's easy digestibility. She's got sharp little teeth that need Carnation's *extra* reinforcement, through irradiation, with "sunshine" vitamin D. And she's got a red-in-the-face temper that's *insulted* by anything tasting less good than this famous milk.

Why experiment? A tall can of Carnation takes one red point, out of Baby's own ration book. Almost any doctor will tell you that you couldn't spend it better. They *know!* They've seen thousands and thousands of babies thrive—on pure, wholesome Carnation.

Plenty of things are uncertain in our topsy-turvy world. Let's stick to one thing you can be sure of. Little children . . . and big ones, too . . . *do well on Carnation!*

This posture was voted **Most Likely to Result in Shrieking, Minor Blood Loss, and Cursing Mixed with Pleas for Forgiveness** in the hotly contested 1944 poll. The very idea of putting a wriggly child on a flat, level surface while you attempt to pierce its garments with a sharp object seems to have eluded Dad. Then again, he just may be confused by the fact that he's putting a diaper on a four-year-old. The kid's probably capable of conversation: *Hey, Pa! Nice tie. How was work? Sorry about the feces, old chum.*

Note the World War II tone of the text: "Plenty of things are uncertain in our topsy-turvy world. Let's stick to one thing you can be sure of. Little children."

Oh, he'll stick the child, all right.

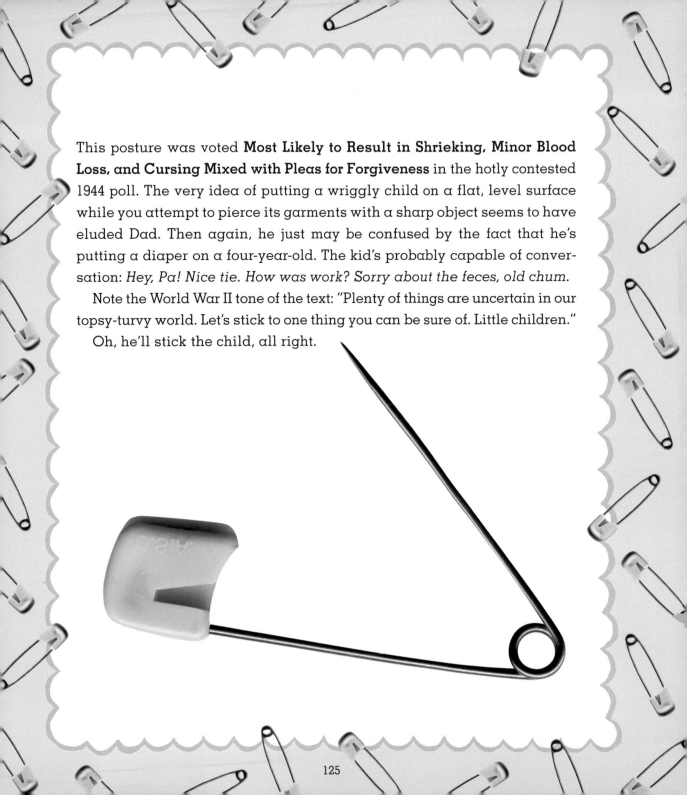

I WANT TO CALL MY DADDY...

Well, now, wait a minute, Junior. Those wires to Washington and to places where they make guns and tanks and planes are crowded with war calls.

OH—I'M SORRY! I FORGOT.

A really necessary call, like to Grandma or Granddad when they are sick, of course, is okay . . . but you wouldn't want to hold up a Long Distance call that might be ordering things for a ship or submarine or fighter plane, now would you?

**GEE, NO—I'LL WAIT TILL
DADDY GETS HOME TO TELL HIM
MY BIG SISTER'S GOT A FELLA.**

Junior, you're a real team-mate. You think like most Americans. They are glad to help by not making Long Distance calls unless they must. And that does the heart good.

BELL TELEPHONE SYSTEM

Here we have the role of a father in wartime: out of town and out of the loop. Before you call your dad for some trivial little nonsense, stop and think, kid: Is Dad located in a city that produces weaponry? If so, hang up! When you call Dad, Tojo smiles!

A necessary call — say, telling Dad that his aged parents got broadsided by a bus yesterday — well, that's okay, but keep in mind that someone may be trying to call the President and tell him they've invented the atomic bomb, and if they get a busy signal, the war will go on long enough for you to see action. You wouldn't want to lose the war in the Pacific, would you? Of course not.

So put that phone down. Wait until he gets home to tell him his daughter has taken up with some 4-F wolf in a zoot suit who smacks his gum and calls your big sister "dolly" and grabs her bottom when your mom's not looking. He can wait.

Someone might be ordering things for a ship.

Clothing & Accessories

Amusements for Children of Bygone Eras

Sharp metal, brittle plastic, flammable fabrics, lethal car seats — it's a wonder anyone made it to puberty without socially debilitating facial scars. This is the sort of stuff that makes you suspect the company behind the Robin Hood Junior Archer Kit also has a profitable line of Li'l Mister Eyepatches. Are you up on your tetanus shots? Then let's continue.

A high chair, c. 1930. Parents were advised to retrofit the chair with four slats, nailed to the legs in the manner shown here. Careful parents also secured the chair to the floor with a nail gun and sloshed a gallon of epoxy around the legs just to be safe. Why? Because otherwise baby would thrash around with the ecstatic abandon most commonly associated with St. Vitus's dance, and knock the chair over.

The child seems to be channeling some horrid demon — *Boo, Mommy! I have come to eat your soul! Please mash it up so I don't choke, okay? I love you. And SATAN!*

WET BEDS?

STAYDRY* PANTY

protects your child
and you against them

$1.95 & up

Expense and discomfort of
rubber sheets gone forever

WHAT IS STAYDRY

STAYDRY prevents discomfort
from wet outer-clothes and wet
bedding. All in one complete
garment.

ACCLAIMED!

. . . acclaimed by thousands
of enthusiastic mothers . . .
praised by many leading doctors. The panty that assures
complete sleeping comfort . . .

STAYDRY (not a diaper) is made
of the finest, highly absorbent material with waterproof outer-covering
of soft, non-toxic plastic . . . can be
worn under pajamas. Requires no
pins. Ties with cloth tape.

NON-BINDING • WASHABLE
BLEACHABLE • BOILABLE

Infants sm. med. lg. (up to 1½ yr.)
$1.95 Waist sizes
18, 20, 22, 24............$3.95
26, 28, 30, 32............$4.95
34, 36, 38, 40............$6.95

Exact waist measurement in inches
necessary for perfect fit, 10% dis-
count when ordering three or more.
Complete satisfaction or Money Back!

COMMENDED
CONSUMER
SERVICE BUREAU
OF
PARENTS'
MAGAZINE
AS ADVERTISED THEREIN

*Reg.
U.S. Pat.

ACCLAIMED BY THOUSANDS!

Mom brought out this ad to show all the girlfriends he brought home from college. He never did marry. Oh, there was that one time he seemed close to popping the question, but for some reason he headed up to the bell tower with a sniper rifle instead.

They're boilable! The ad assures us it's "not a diaper." No, it's a panty! Great: That's a distinction the Bully-American community is sure to grasp.

You think today's children are obese? The waist size on these things went up to 40 inches.

It's the Habitutor™, the good habit builder that makes it fun to be good and good to be fun, habitually. Translation: Some creepy clown crap that will peer at your child from the darkened bathroom, taunting him with his garish soundless maw. It's unclear how this is an "amazing new idea," but it's also not apparent how placing an implement of dental hygiene into the plastic claw of an itinerant mime can make "brushing teeth fun." Unless he amuses himself by snapping the head off the brush now and then, or making the toothpaste ooze bloodred while calling the kid's name in a guttural moan. And even that stretches the definition of "fun."

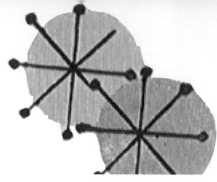

a festive note for spring...
the TINY TOURIST group by TRAVEL HEIR
with matching covers

To travel in style, here's the TINY TOURIST pattern by TRAVEL HEIR
available in seat, bed, and portable walker. The matching covers are
quality crafted, heavily quilted and fully waterproofed. Modern design
consists of pink, blue, pearl gray and gold printed on white background.

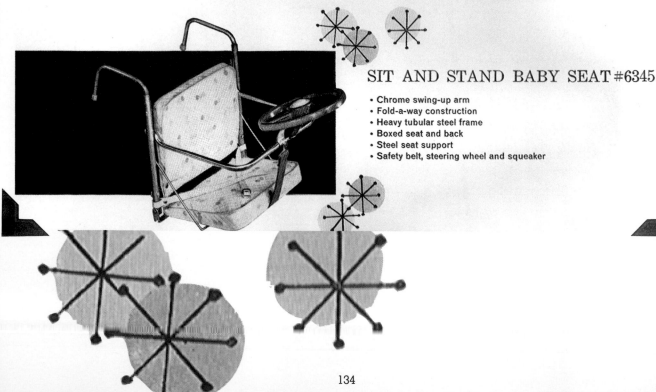

SIT AND STAND BABY SEAT #6345

- Chrome swing-up arm
- Fold-a-way construction
- Heavy tubular steel frame
- Boxed seat and back
- Steel seat support
- Safety belt, steering wheel and squeaker

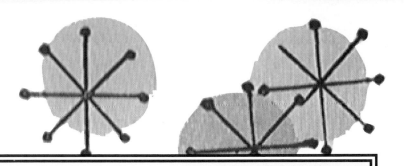

And you're likely to be heirborne, should Mom ever slam on the brakes. It's not exactly bolted in place, is it?

Then again, I come from the era when children rode in the front seat, facing a sharp metal dashboard tailor-made for decapitation, held in place by nothing more than melted thigh-skin adhering to the hot vinyl seat covers. How did we survive? Mom's right arm. For many generations, a mom simply knew that when she had to brake quickly, one hand should shoot over and brace the child. A good mom could do this while hydroplaning, braking, and checking her mascara in the rearview mirror. It was an instinct so deeply bred that my mom was still giving me karate chops in the sternum when I was in eleventh grade.

The current baby seat is much superior to these devises: Well padded, lightweight, so safe you could hit a wall doing Mach 3 and the kid would burp, at most. But just try to give a used one away. Our local charities kindly decline the offer, fearing the legal repercussions should the seat malfunction somehow, so everyone either passes them along or throws them away. When the archaeologists of the future plow through our landfills, they'll find a thick, chunky layer of plastic car seats, but no Tiny Tourists. They were all melted down for ammo for the Vietnam War.

They won't harm Baby even if he puts them in his mouth. It's a safe white. Yes, this lead-based polish is triple-distilled for purity!

Baby looks as though he's half an hour into a bad trip brought on by shoe-polish huffing. *Whoahhh, man, shoes. Didja ever think about shoes, man? They're freakin' me out.* But don't worry: They're the safest shoe tinter available. A model in a nurse's hat says so. We're also assured that the polish gets rid of messy greasy spots, which is great if you dress Baby in his Sunday best and use him to swab out the deep-fat fryer.

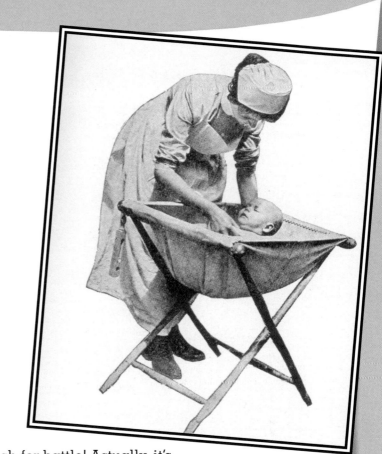

Florence Nightingale visits a World War I frontline nursery and makes a new recruit fresh for battle! Actually, it's just a demonstration for the modern home bath of 1917. Mother is wearing a "bathing apron," also known as the 47th layer of clothing women had to wear back then; her cap keeps her hair neat and prevents stray follicles from contaminating the bathwater. (Which was presumably drawn from the horse's trough.) The bathtub itself is a rather casual affair, and the goal would seem to be the frantic, speedy washing of the infant before the water seeped completely through the cloth.

The design won the award for most Likely to Be Knocked Over by the Dog. Basic, simple, easy. Surely science could improve on the device, no?

NEW BABY BATH STYLING

TRIMBLE'S *Kiddie-Bath*® SUPREME

This new Kiddie-Bath has the style, sturdiness and convenience to appeal to mother, dad, baby and grandma. An attractive piece of furniture, with polished aluminum upright legs for strength and mobility. Rolls easily from room to room on plastic casters. Comes equipped with the Baby-Form tub, guard rails on three sides, play balls, drain hose, safety strap, Tufflex pillow, solid aluminum table, 18" deep rim utility tray, 2 roomy side trays.

MOLDED BABY-FORM® TUB

WITH BUILT-IN TUB REST...

AVAILABLE ON 4 TRIMBLE KIDDIE-BATH MODELS

The tub rest is molded right in. No extra parts to arrange, adjust or clean. Tub lifts out easily for filling or emptying, or attached drain hose with clamp can be used. Removable foam rubber pillow. Tub has many household uses and is ideal for travel.

All purpose use in bath, kitchen, nursery. Has many household uses after baby graduates to adult tub.

TRIMBLE FREIGHT COSTS ARE DEDUCTIBLE on orders of $100 or more at no increase in most prices. Merchandise shipped F.O.B. plant.

TRIMBLE INC., ROCHESTER 13, N.Y.

TRIMBLE

138

New and Improved Baby Bath

Depends what you mean by "improved." This looks more like a device for extracting confessions, frankly. They probably sold a thousand of these to East Germany, with car batteries mounted to the bottom. Rolls on casters from cell to cell!

The tub is contained under the changing table — and if we may, a word about that mattress. Anyone who grew up post-Ike knows the feeling of that cold plastic material under our bare butt — the sullen and resentful way it refused to mold to your weight, the raspy scalloped edge where the elastic bunched up. The pillow, according to the ad copy, is made of "Tufflex." Yes, you want *Tufflex* in a pillow, given the notorious tendency of babies to excrete corrosive acids through their scalps. The arrangement of the play balls is interesting, and would suggest it was designed for infant babies with four arms on their left side.

Well, who knew what nuclear testing would wind up causing. Plan ahead; it's the American way. And it's easier now with Tufflex!

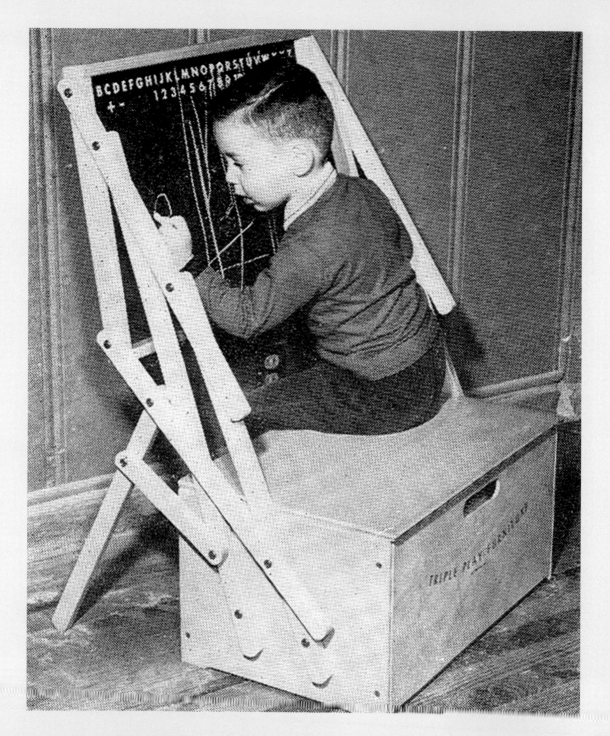

The "Triple Play Furniture" Fun-Set, c. 1960.

Your choice:

1. Dad set it up. It doesn't look like anything on the box. To hell with it.

2. The result of a well-funded multi-year government study to develop a toy that had the maximum potential for pinching your finger.

3. Marcel Duchamp's card table.

4. An alien being that sat silent for weeks, waiting for the moment when it could spring to life and deposit the child in the box below, where digestion was swift and certain.

One hates to break it to the fine folks at Wonderland, but the idea that something is an animal, a vehicle, AND a bank does not represent some brilliant imaginative synthesis. It's just damn confusing, and that's all.

"I'm Caw Caw the Taxi — but I'm different from all the other taxis. I'm a crow and a taxi and a bank. "Uh-huh, pal. *Sure* you are. Why don't you have a seat. I'll call J. D. Rockefeller and tell him you're ready to fly home.

These boring multiple-personality statuettes were intended to help kids "develop calm, peaceful, educational play habits and encourage thrift," preparing them for a life as a Zen Master Bank President. They accomplish these goals while "'disarming' the little folk from playthings that glorify violence." But we all know what happened: Some kid in a Hopalong Cassidy outfit jacked the crow for his coins, after which the boys had ramming contests that left the toys scuffed and busted.

"My back is a bank and a convertible automobile, the rest of me is a turtle."

Nowadays they can correct that with surgery.

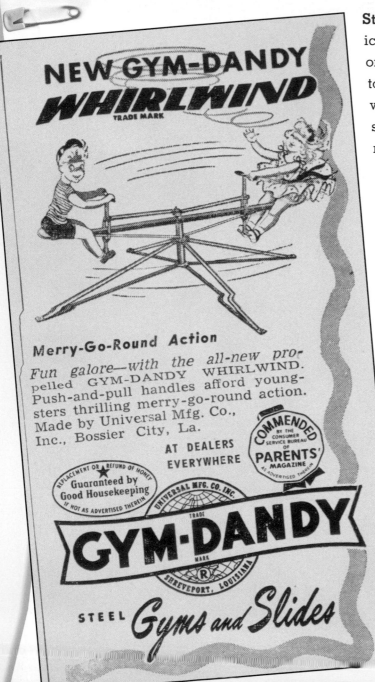

Step one: Put some beer on ice, Mom. Dad's going to need one after he puts this thing together. Note how it wobbles when he's done. Note how he shrugs. Light a cigarette and repress your contempt.

Step two: Shave the kids' heads. It'll make it easier when they go in for stitches later today.

Step three: Skip lunch. Save time and pour the Beefaroni right on the ground, since that's where it will end up anyway.

Step four: Sue the Universal Mfg. Co. Oh, right: It's 1955. No one does that. Yet.

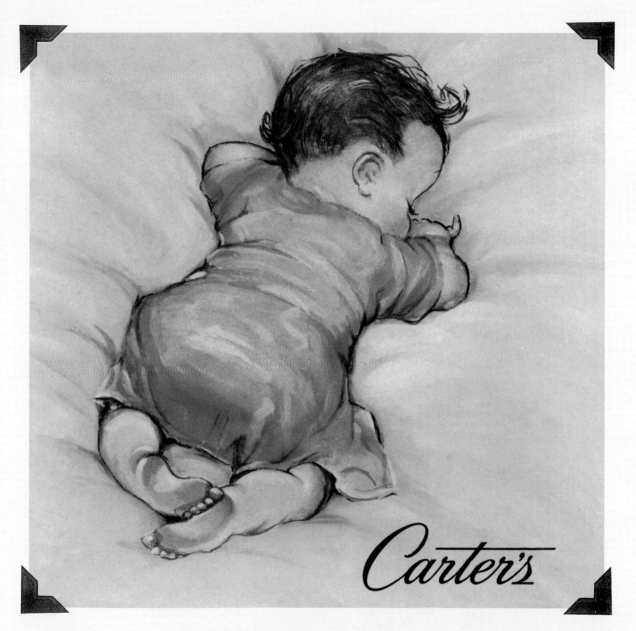

Carter's

A sleepwear box, c. 1958. Recommended posture for naps: facedown! Right now in bookstores across America, hundreds of modern parents are instinctively pawing the page, *trying to turn the baby over.*

Now this, ladies and gentlemen, is a 1950s pediatrician. Or a priest in a mummy movie; could go either way. He has the authoritative bulk, the peering eyes that can diagnose your bedwetting just by looking at you, the round mirror on his head for which no convincing explanation is ever given, and — of course — the hairy forearms. Because nothing says 1950s pediatrician like the hairy forearms. Except perhaps the GIGANTIC HANDS.

As the ad shows, he is also capable of speaking without moving his lips.

You think he knows about that time you showed the neighbor girl your pee-pee? Of course he does.

And he's going to tell your pastor.

An oversized Kennedy-head grafted onto a small human. But if that seems unnatural, consider the particulars of the garment. It's made of rugged Dantwill, Sanforized and vat-dyed, Zelan water resistant. Might as well dip the kid in a slurry of DDT and asbestos.

Also available in tweed and herringbone, for when your little boy is playing with the Windsors.

Nine, er, out of, er, ten, ah, budding John F. Kennedy imperson-atahs prefer the vigah of Miami knitting mill clothing!

THE **LEATHER** IS **THERE** IN EVERY PAIR

...That's Why Peters Children's Shoes Fit Better, Look Better, AND GIVE **MILES** OF EXTRA WEAR!

Whether you're trying to thrash a close friend to impress a gal, or laughing at his pathetic attempts, or merely practicing for the day when you'll start fights in pool halls by flirting with everyone and then standing back to watch the roosters go at one another while you blow smoke rings with bemused contentment, remember: **Without leather, life itself would be impossible.**

Too bad science wasn't around when the kid did a header out of this thing. **What's missing in the Babytron?** (Aside from some incredibly futuristic date like BABYTRON 1980, for the INFANT OF TOMORROW!) Right: a seat belt. Yes, the patented Babytron technology permits children to slide down the modern, scientific way and clip their chins on the sheet-metal tray the scientific, modern way. They might even catch the footstep on the way down. If you don't think that can happen, you don't know babies; dip them in epoxy and line the chair with coarse sandpaper, and they'll still slip out like mercury going through a duck's digestive system. The ad copy insists that the device is "insured against tipping" — which just may mean the company took out a big policy to pay off the inevitable suits. It also "cleans in a jiffy," which is nice if you happen to live in a jiffy, but those who live in a house will soon realize that mashed bananas, yogurt, applesauce, and macaroni bond with any child's high chair at the subatomic level, and cannot be dislodged without high-pressure water hoses of the type used to put out fires on the seventh floor of a high-rise.

Babytron

The chair that science built

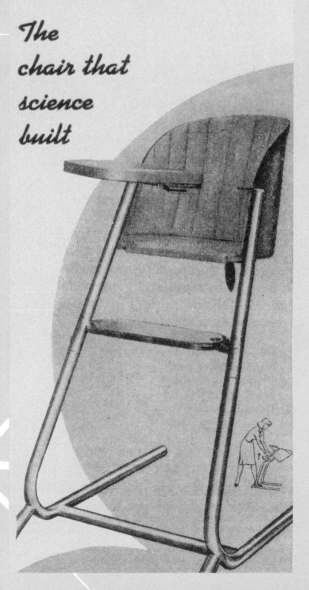

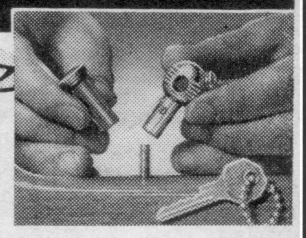

Yes, you would want to prevent this. It's such an annoyance. At least these parents have noticed that Junior's toppled out the back door; oftentimes you don't know until it just seems quieter than usual back there. And where's that breeze coming from? Oh, for heaven's sake. Henry, turn around — Junior threw himself out on the turnpike again.

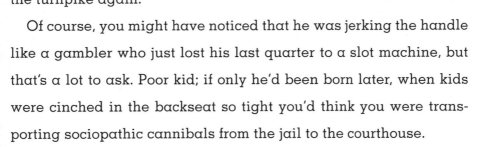

Of course, you might have noticed that he was jerking the handle like a gambler who just lost his last quarter to a slot machine, but that's a lot to ask. Poor kid; if only he'd been born later, when kids were cinched in the backseat so tight you'd think you were transporting sociopathic cannibals from the jail to the courthouse.

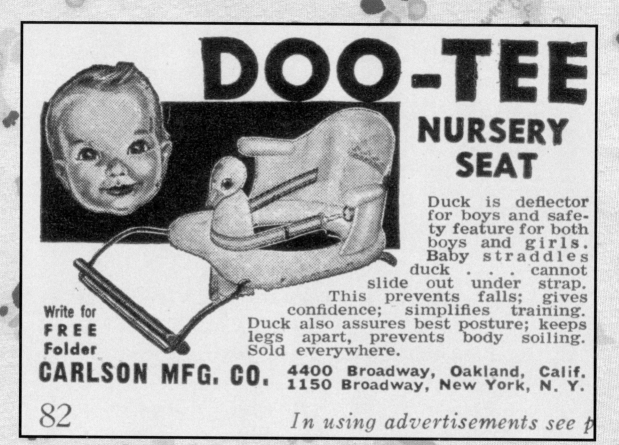

DOO-TEE
NURSERY
SEAT

Duck is deflector for boys and safety feature for both boys and girls. Baby straddles duck . . . cannot slide out under strap. This prevents falls; gives confidence; simplifies training. Duck also assures best posture; keeps legs apart, prevents body soiling. Sold everywhere.

Write for
FREE
Folder

CARLSON MFG. CO. 4400 Broadway, Oakland, Calif.
1150 Broadway, New York, N. Y.

82

In using advertisements see p

Doo-tee, Honor, Country

Another example of the strap-'em-and-leave-'em school, this device let Baby sprawl boneless in his chair while a hollowed-out waterfowl decoy reflected the pounding stream into the basin. The assertion that the "duck also assures best posture" is rather fanciful, as is the assurance that the duck "gives confidence."

"Senator! You have the manner and bearing of a man who has mastered this strange play of shadow and light we call life; to what do you credit your confidence?"

"I peed inside a duckhead for a few months. Next question!"

Baby Always Comes Along

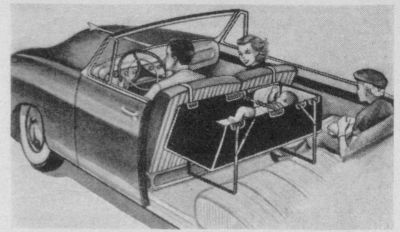

in His Safe, Comfortable...

car-baby
Reg. U. S. Pat. Off.

convertible
by *Bunny Bear*

A BED IN FRONT OR BACK

A SEAT IN FRONT OR BACK

Every trip is fun for baby and mother with the genuine "Car Baby". Converts from cozy crib to comfortable seat in a jiffy. And versatile! "Car Baby" can be used "cross-car", or with front leg extension when three are riding in front. For beach, porch or overnight visits too. Both body and plastic mattress are water repellent. About $8.98 — slightly higher West. Only "Car Baby" fits all cars. Insist on the original.

WRITE FOR FREE BOOKLET AND NEAREST STORE.

BUNNY BEAR, 3 NURSERY LANE, EVERETT 49, MASSACHUSETTS

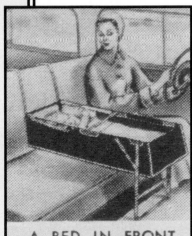

A BED IN FRONT OR BACK

This seems to take the idea of a "convertible" a bit too far; the entire rear portion of the car has been removed, so baby and a devalued elderly relative can ride along exposed to the elements. This design has the patented "auto-fling" feature that guarantees maximum altitude no matter how fast Daddy drives the car into a tree.

In short: The idea of tying the seat down never seems to have occurred to them. It's almost as if everyone had agreed to discourage seat belts —which, after all, might give people the idea there was something inherently dangerous about driving seventy miles an hour with nothing to stop them but a pointy chrome steering column. Might as well have titled the ads "Don't Let YOUR Child Be an Orphan" and be done with it.

A SEAT IN FRONT OR BACK

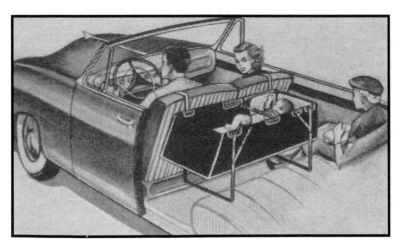

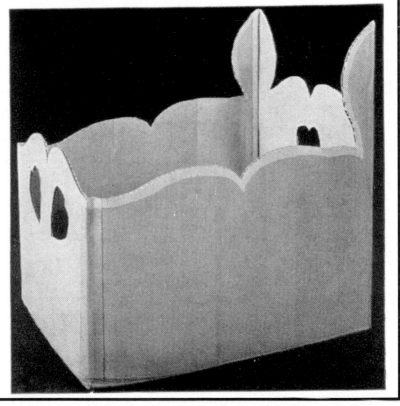

FIG. 48. An improvised bed made from a corrugated carton by an ingenious father. Note ventilators for air and high points to permit use of a netting during insect season.

Presenting the ingenious cardboard baby bed. Now with air holes!

Why? Because people are more likely to accept a baby left on their doorstep if it's in a box that vaguely recalls a bunny. Ring the bell, arrange the netting — it's insect season, after all — and run. To ensure a good first impression, paint the sides to remove the name of the liquor manufacturer.

It's board-soft for extra **comfort!** Helps straighten weak spines. All-American design ensures the seat can be leaned against any wall or couch or shin of a slumbering vagrant in the next bus seat. Freezes baby in a posture of astonishment. Simplifies infant care somehow; details not provided on request. Designed by a baby doctor. Well, a doctor. In Mexico. Who works with babies. Okay, puppies. Jeez.

FOR INFANTS
up to 12 MONTHS

TESTED AND COMMENDED by PARENTS' MAGAZINE CONSUMER SERVICE BUREAU

Designed by a baby doctor. For feeding, carrying, exercise, and for travel in car, train, plane or bus. Simplifies and facilitates infant care. At leading stores, or write today for pictorial circular.

INFANSEAT

INFANSEAT CO.
DES MOINES, IOWA   DEPT. P

They don't actually clean themselves, since that would imply they were both alive and intelligent. Many a mother would be relieved to wake one night and find the nursing bottles cleaning themselves, marching around the counter like the enchanted broomsticks of *The Sorcerer's Apprentice*, but after a while they'd creep you out something fierce. Then again, if you had a baby like this one, you'd be used to all manner of flesh-crawling sights. Of course, nowadays we can test for the Thirties Hooker Gene early in the womb. The secret to the Brushless Baby Bottle Cleanser is not revealed, except to note its "special penetrating action" — which, of course, got you in this mess in the first place. There's still a Puritan Chemical Company, incidentally; they make hydrochloric acid, ammonium hydroxide, and Red Fuming Nitric Acid. Well, someone has to. In retrospect, it's possible the substance cleaned the bottles by dissolving them entirely.

STOP BRUSHING BABY BOTTLES!

NEW PRODUCT ENDS THIS CHORE · · · ·

At last! Nursing Bottles clean themselves with

PURITAN BRUSHLESS BABY BOTTLE CLEANSER

Works like magic! Simply add a spoonful of Puritan Brushless Baby Bottle Cleanser to a gallon of water . . . nursing bottles will soak clean without fuss or bother! And they're spotless and sparkling; free from any soapy film! The secret of this cleanser's efficiency is its special penetrating action that gets under milk residue to remove it! Mild, pure, perfectly harmless!

* Cleans without brushing!
* Its penetrating action gets under milk residue!
* Will not injure nipples!
* Pure and Harmless!

FREE SAMPLE:

Try it yourself; send us your name for a free sample of Puritan Brushless Baby Bottle Cleanser.

PURITAN CHEMICAL COMPANY
Atlanta, Georgia

2 Sizes. 49c and 79c

COMMENDED PARENTS MAGAZINE CONSUMER SERVICE BUREAU

Puritan
BRUSHLESS
BABY BOTTLE
Cleanser

The Bucking Bronco Cowboy Horse Real Live Pony was not as realistic as the ad suggests. As every parent knows, the Real Live Ponies you encounter at county fairs are docile and sweet, thanks to the pop-bottle-sized barbiturate suppositories their owners employ before letting the kids hop on their backs and dig their heels into the animals' tender sides. The Real Live Pony trots around with the telltale *dude, whatever* expression of a horse who knows his lot in life is to have his velvety ears yanked for five hours, followed by a nice bag of oats and the sweet release of dreamless sleep. This pony is a MANIAC. It bobs up and down and up and down and back and forth as though it had digested some psychosis-inducing mold. If Real Live Ponies behaved like this one, no one would have ever dared domesticate the things. Run! It is the loco bucking devil-cow! Run for your lives!

According to the ad, the Bucking Bronco Cowboy Horse "stays in one spot no matter how hard he's ridden," which is nonsense; every kid managed to cross the rumpus room in this thing. If you rode it down hard and jerked it up fast, you could make it jump half an inch off the floor, and that's when you threw your weight into it, simultaneously pulling it up with your hands. Eventually, the rug would gather under your steed's steel bars, and you'd have to dismount — but that was easier said than done. Picture a block of wood suspended from four corners by springs. Picture yourself bobbing up and down on the block. Now get off. Oh: You're two years old and have the coordination of an arthritic sloth. Take it from there.

More Than a Little Stranger

It's the "Build Your Own Baby Martin Luther Kit," complete with a Smiting Mitre that doubles as a bubble wand.

This hails from a 1926 guide for upper-class moms that referred to babies as "the little stranger," which was a term of endearment in those days. Technically, it's true, but it still suggests that Flapper Era moms looked down at the squalling little thing who'd burst from their womb and wondered, Now, who the hell are you?

Pillow
4-26-393

Coat
4-26-39

Dress

There was a great vogue for matching outfits in the 1940s. Moms could make them out of the same pattern. But in this case, Mom used her creativity to assemble her daughters out of a variety of body parts, scavenged perhaps from the graveyard. The older sister appears to have the head of a 40-year-old woman who expired from drinking Sterno, and the smaller child a head equal in size to her entire torso. But they look great in a Cinderella Frock! It hides the stitches.

Of the several thousand people on whom the Army tested LSD, only one went into children's sleepwear.

Not all rooms need be traditional: This handy organizing space is useful for parents who are raising their children in a sound stage. Or for those busy moms who must monitor secret wavelengths from Planet X in case the Meltrons announce they are returning for the young

Zorgo, the sole survivor of a saucer crash on the planet called Earth. We hope you have been boiling the synthetic breast-nozzle replacement, Human Female.

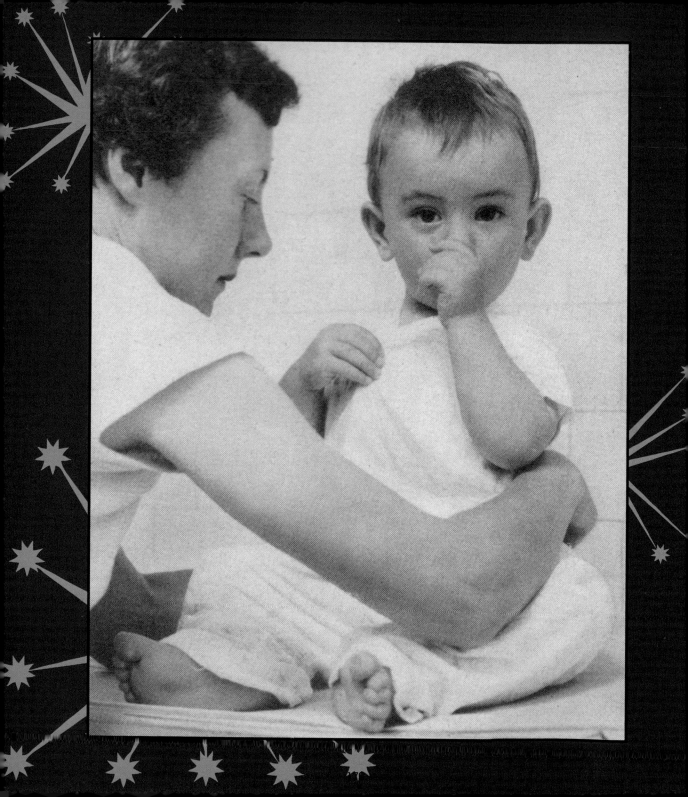

You lookin' at me? You lookin' at *me*? Because I don't see anyone else here. Granted, I can't exactly focus very well, but I detect the indistinct outline of someone meeting my challenging stare.

And you don't want that to happen. Luckily, science came up with several substances that could break the onerous habit.

Thum ("We removed the *B* and passed the savings along to you!") was a god-send for mothers whose child didn't just suck his thumb but hoovered up his thumbs, plural, pausing only to gnaw off a nail. Stop him now before he hits bone! Thum used the comforting analogue of nail polish to reassure moms that this stuff was utterly safe. Main ingredient: capsicum, also known as the stuff that makes Tabasco light up your mouth and send a sluice of jittery fire down your intestinal tubes. Add a dash of isopropyl and some acetone, and what mom wouldn't say yes? Also good as a varnish stripper or condiment for "Mexican Night" suppers, provided this Mexican night took place in a paint factory or an auto-body detailing shop.

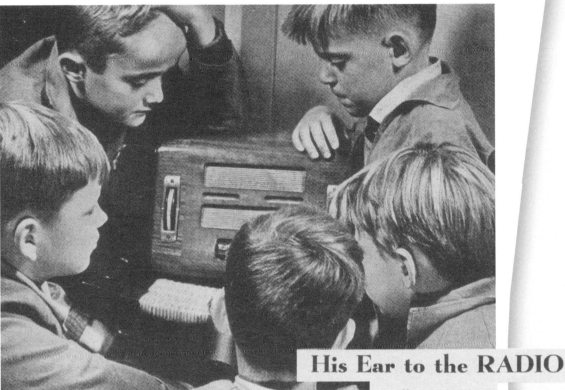

His Ear to the RADIO

Many parents are disturbed by their children's taste in radio programs. What should they do about it?

What should parents do? They should lie back, close their eyes, and imagine an era in which televisions are the size of garage doors and display all manner of dismemberment and explicit sex, viewed by their children with slack-jawed amazement while they're at work. Compared to that, listening to a radio show seems rather tame, no matter how much gunplay comes through the tinny little speaker.

If one can judge from the illustration, there's nothing to worry about, since the Youth of Today appear to favor shows that help them learn how to make the right faces during a funeral.

Dibrom-oxymercuri-fluorescein-sodium — ask for it by name! Any kid who grew up in the Annette Funicello era remembers this stuff. Mercurochrome: You know it works, because it stings like hell. Mommy, I have a cut, and it hurts! Well, let me magnify the pain by a factor of ten, then. Let's see . . . where did I put the caustic lye? Ah well, have to use old dependable dibrom-oxymercuri-fluorescein-sodium. Roll up your sleeve, dear. Bite down on this piece of leather while I clean the wound.

Finally...

Baby Care in Simple Terms

TO MOTHER

You dry 'em (like dishes)

You scrub 'em (like floors)

You wrap 'em (like mummies) For going outdoors.

TO FATHER

You oil 'em (like motors)

You change 'em (like tires)

You constantly stoke 'em (Like tendin' to fires).

TO BOTH

You pet 'em (like puppies)—You love 'em (like mad!) And they bring you more joy—than you EVER HAVE HAD!

News Flash! Babies need clothes! Here's a helpful hint: If it's snowing outside, think ceremonial burial shroud for skeletal Egyptian royalty. That'll help you remember. In addition to clothes, babies also need coal, motor oil on the buttocks, and to be petted like puppies.

Anyone who needs these things explained in these terms *should not be breeding*.